STO

**ACPL ITEM
DISCARDED**

SO-EBR-840

3-25-74

**HOW TO CHOOSE
YOUR VACATION
HOUSE**

Bruce Cassiday

HOW TO CHOOSE YOUR VACATION HOUSE

Illustrated with photographs and diagrams

DODD, MEAD & COMPANY
New York

PICTURE CREDITS

The illustrations that appear in this book are used by courtesy of:

Acorn Structures, Inc., pages 10, 100, 103, 105; Aladdin Company, 96; American Plywood Association, 4, 15, 18, 21, 34, 35, 36, 38, 39, 41, 42, 43, 46, 48, 49, 136, 137, 140, 144, 145, 165, 170, 171, 172, 192, 193, 194, 195, 207, 218; Andersen Windows, 187; Armstrong Information Center, 129 (top left, top right), 132 (top left, top right, bottom), 133, 134, 203; Bruce Company, 202; Burkin Homes, Inc., 132 (middle); California Redwood Association, 8, 186, 280; Great Northern Homes, 100; Homelite, 241; International Homes of Cedar, 78, 79; K Products Corporation, 82, 83; Lindal Cedar Homes, 66, 67, 68; Lumber Enterprises, Inc., 72, 73; Marlite Paneling, 204; Masonite Corporation, 200, 231; Mobile Homes, 109, 110, 112, 118, 120, 123, 124; National Homes, Inc., 116; National Lumber Manufacturers Association, 164; National Paint & Coatings Association, 214; Pease Company, 94; Ponderosa Pine Woodwork, 173, 174, 175, 176, 177, 178; Red Cedar Shingle & Handsplit Shake Bureau, 12, 190, 211; Shelter-Kit, Inc., 61, 62, 63, 64; Sumner Rider Associates, 186, 196, 197; U. S. Department of Agriculture, 233, 237, 244, 245, 248, 249, 257, 262, 263, 266; Ward Cabin Company, 74, 75; Wausau Homes, Inc., 88, 89; Western Wood Products Association, 123, 124, 147, 154, 155, 168, 179, 180, 181, 182, 224, 225, 226, 227, 268, 272, 274, 277, 278, 280, 283, 286; Weston Homes, Inc., 98; Westville Homes, Inc., 129 (middle, bottom)

Photographs which are reproduced through the courtesy of: Anthony's Studio, pages 129; Becker Creative Photography, 88, 89; Better Homes & Gardens, 187; Ed Dull, 272, 283; Walter Hagemann, 8; Phokion Karas, 186, 187; Lisanti, Inc., 137; Marten Photo, 165; Charles Pearson, 286; Richards Studios, 66, 67, 78, 79; Karl H. Riek, 211; Fred Rola, 277; Bob Towers, 21, 48, 49; Les Turnau, 190.

Copyright© 1974 by Bruce Cassiday
All rights reserved
No part of this book may be reproduced in any form without permission in writing from the publisher

ISBN: 0-396-06813-8
Library of Congress Catalog Card Number: 73-3903
Printed in the United States of America

1790588

ACKNOWLEDGMENTS

I would like to express my personal thanks to the following people and organizations for their help in making this book possible:

Dave Rogoway, American Plywood Association; Larry M. Coy III, California Redwood Association; Merlin Blais, Western Wood Products Association; Franklin C. Welch and Dick Lee for the Red Cedar Shingle & Handsplit Shake Bureau; Beth M. Mathes, National Paint and Coatings Association; Hildegarde Popper, Sumner Rider Associates; Marguaretta M. Hedge, Information Service Branch, U.S. Department of Agriculture, Agricultural Research Service; Ralph Rittenour, Home Building Plan Service; W. D. Gaittens, Western Wood Moulding and Millwork Producers; John R. Malmo for E. L. Bruce Company; Leonard Ansell for Homelite; Leo Floros for Masonite Corporation; Gilbert Dean for International Homes of Cedar; F. Michael Peringer for Lindal Cedar Homes; Armstrong Information Service; and Marlite Paneling.

CONTENTS

1. Where to Build	1
2. Plywood Construction	26
3. Precut Construction	53
4. Interlock Construction	69
5. Prefabricated Construction	85
6. Mobile Homes	107
7. Modular Construction	127
8. Custom Construction	135
9. Building Tips	158
10. Designs and Styles	183
11. Painting	205
12. Built-ins	223
13. Heating	228
14. Utilities	239
15. Sanitation	256
16. Landscaping	269
17. Winterizing	287
18. Financing and Insurance	294
Appendix	
Manufacturers of Vacation Houses	305
Vacation House Plans	306
Index	307

Prices of vacation houses quoted in this book have been estimated as closely as possible to the current rate of construction costs. However, figures vary from region to region, and will certainly rise in the coming months.

BRUCE CASSIDAY

Chapter 1

WHERE TO BUILD

THE location for your leisure home can be almost as important as the construction of the house itself. The search for that perfect building site can be a troublesome experience, for there are many stumbling blocks to trip up the unwary and change a leisure home from a dream to a nightmare.

The site of your second home is of far greater significance than the site of your first house. The locale of the second home is all-important; the structure is subordinate. For that reason, you should decide exactly where you want to build before you make any other plans.

Over the years, several important rules of thumb have been drawn up by generations of second-home real estate buyers. They can help expose hidden flaws in bad locations that may look perfect as well as uncover inherent advantages in sites that you might ordinarily pass up.

Broadly speaking, there are essentially five different kinds of recreational areas in which you might want to build a second home: seaside, lakeside, countryside, mountainside, and snow and ski.

SEASIDE

The seashores of every country in the world are dotted with cabins, houses, and palatial mansions. The allure of sea and shore has always called to people of all means: there is swimming, body-surfing, surfboarding; seashells for the finding, beaches for combing; sailing for mariners, and fish to be caught.

Houses built along saltwater shores, from cabins up to the most expensive structures imaginable, tend to be flat buildings whose low profiles minimize the structural damage caused by high winds. Most of them are left unpainted to weather naturally, for saltwater breaks down paint pigmentation much faster than fresh water. Seaside homes should be designed to be snug on nights when the seas are kicking up and storm clouds are closing down over the land.

At the seashore there is the same variability of weather a sailor experiences on board a ship: balmy days, days of deep doldrums, hot days, breezy days, nippy days, cold days, rainy days, windy days, stormy days, and bitterly chill days. The ideal seashore house should be built to withstand any kind of weather.

In choosing a seaside homesite, you are necessarily limited to available space. But there are certain considerations that are important. They concern the three categories of hazards to guard against: hurricanes and high winds; sand and rock erosion; and tidal conditions.

Hurricanes and high-velocity winds strike seashores all over the world. If the sites you are looking at have long stretches of sand in front of them, choose one with a good high sand dune that is matted solidly with dune grass and other plantings. A dune that is not anchored will blow away and could even be a hazard to the house you intend to build. Hurricanes blow not only sand and rain at the house, but seawater as well. Protection of any kind—rocks, piers, earthworks, dunes—will save you much upkeep and maintenance.

Sand erosion can be a danger no matter in which direction it moves. If tidal conditions are drawing the sand in front of the site out to sea, avoid the area; soon the sand will be drawn from your front door, leaving you in the ocean. If the sand is being blown away in back of the site, you may one day be left high and dry all around and will be in danger of sinking into the sea too.

In certain localities, sand erosion is not the only problem. Sometimes solid earth and rock tend to break off and drift away in heavy tides. Even cliffs composed of rock may crumble away under the constant battering of sea, wind, and rain. It is not wise to buy a site where there is any evidence of such geological instability.

Tidal damage usually leaves clear marks where it has occurred. Check into the history of the beach area in which you are interested to see if there is any previous history of tidal damage.

Ice plants and bunch grass keep sand from blowing away and leaving this house stranded and open to buffeting of wind and sea.

Your best bet is to choose a lot in a section with plenty of jetties that extend out into the sea. Sometimes communities erect breakwaters to cut down on beach erosion; such areas are usually good risks. You can tell a lot by looking at other houses nearby; note how they have weathered wind, sand, and water.

As for insurance for water damage—forget it. It is either nonexistent or at such a high premium as to be out of the question. You must select the site of your seashore home so that you will be subject to the least water damage possible.

LAKESIDE

The lakes that stud the mountain areas of America have always attracted owners of second houses. Not only can you swim, but you can ride a powerboat, water-ski, row a skiff, operate a sailboat, and fish to your heart's content.

Unlike seawater, fresh water at a lakeside does not tend to break down paint pigmentation and metal surfaces with the ferocity of saltwater. Nor will the climate of a lake site tend to batter the houses on its shoreline with the intensity of an ocean climate.

However, the possibility of tidal damage is as great on a lakeshore as it is on the seashore. Erosion of the shoreline of sand or rock is a constant danger. In some cases, a lakeshore can be pulled apart much more swiftly by water action than a seashore. It all depends on the lake and its ecological condition.

Flood damage on the shore of a lake can be severe during the season of thaw and the season of heavy rain. It is a good idea to be aware of all seasonal changes and to know how they affect the spot of land in which you are interested.

At a lakefront site there is the possibility of damage by water from two sides—front *and* back. Be sure not to choose a site that looks as if it had once been the bed of a stream, no matter how dry and innocent it may now appear. If a portion of earth has ever once held rushing water, the chances are that it will do so again sometime.

Do not build a house on or near *any* dry creek—onshore or away from it. Be particularly sure not to build at the juncture of a dry creek and a lake; there you will have trouble not only from rushing creek water, but from rising lake water in thaw or flood.

Wind boiling across a lake can fling lake water with great force and velocity. If there is a ten-

dency for the wind to blow in one direction across a lake, pick a site on the lee shore. A house on the windward shore is apt to call for a great deal more maintenance.

Because life on the shore of a lake has a leisurely quality, the site you pick should have large enough land area around it for outdoor living.

In shopping for lakeshore property, look around and see how the neighboring houses have weathered the years. From them you'll get a good indication of what lies in store for your vacation house.

COUNTRYSIDE

In spite of the fact that many people tend to select a homesite either on a seashore or on a lakeshore, there are thousands of square miles

A perfect vacation-house site has plenty of room to enjoy the leisurely life.

of wonderful meadows, valleys, hills, plains, and deserts where you can enjoy solitude and contentment as well as a variety of different kinds of recreational activities.

The beauty of a countryside home is that it is not subject to adverse weather the way a lakeside or seaside home may be. The climate is usually more equable, making for an easier kind of life for the homeowner and a more benign environment for the house itself. Countryside property is often not as expensive as seashore or lakeshore property, and it demands quite a bit less maintenance and care.

In a typical countryside retreat, the craftsmanship of the second home can be much simpler than the exacting workmanship demanded by seashore and lakeshore dwellings. The serenity and harmony of nature can be expressed by simple lines in the house itself.

Look for a site that suits your personal needs—lots of trees; a spectacular view; a rushing stream; a flat, endless desert; a rockbound clifftop; a meadow of wildflowers. It's all up to you; the possibilities are limitless.

One thing you should study with some care is the weather range during the time period you will spend in the house. Learn the direction of the prevailing winds and select your site accordingly. Learn the variability ranges of the seasons and select the site that is at its best at the season you wish to use it. Learn the nature of all the land nearby—is it swampy, dry, rocky?—so that you will be ready to ignore, avoid, or control it if necessary.

The beauty of a countryside home is its versatility; the site you select should reflect this. You

High in the Sierra, this redwood vacation home spans a trout stream. Architect Francis Joseph McCarthy constructed the span across the stream with 48-foot steel beams.

can build as large—or as small—a place as you want. You can add recreational facilities at will: a swimming pool, a tennis court, a baseball diamond, a bowling green. You can landscape it to your heart's content, or you can let nature take its course. Of all the types of vacation houses, the one built on a charming countryside site can be the most rewarding in terms of lifelong contentment and personal pride.

MOUNTAINSIDE

Life in the mountains can be rugged, and you should take this into consideration when choosing a mountain site so as not to make the construction of the house too difficult. When searching for a spot, you can either choose a site where your house will blend into its surroundings so that it cannot be seen, or one where you can build a house that is purposely obtrusive and bright with colors, shapes, and texture.

The main things to remember about a mountain site is that winter weather sometimes can dump snow on it to depths of ten feet or more. Avoid such a site if you want your home to weather the winter months safely.

In site-searching, remember that high land is always preferable to low land, but that *any* land on a mountain slope can be in danger of erosion, landslide, and collapse. Look out for the site above which great ice packs form in the winter, or where incipient glaciers grow. On a mountain slope pay particular attention not only to the site itself, but to what lies above it and below it. Your house can be ruined by rocks and ice hurtling down from above as well as by slides and erosion that pull out the terrain from below.

Winds are rugged in mountainous areas; so are snows, rains, and sleet. Be sure you select a site where your home can be anchored securely into the mountainside. Try to find a natural site in a pocket or on a ledge, making sure that the pocket or ledge is not fault-ridden and so might split apart under geologic stress and demolish your house.

Trees on a mountain site can be a great help

Home is placed in heavily wooded area so that views from main deck and aerie-type windows on second and "attic" levels are not obscured.

in sheltering and protecting the house from the harsh brutalities of weather. So can earth and rock formations. By the same token, trees can also shut off the spectacular view which attracted you to the site in the first place. It is difficult to judge how a house will look nestled in trees and rocks; be very careful that natural obstructions do not cut off important ventilation and sunshine.

Mountain sites have increased in popularity in recent years with the rising interest in backpacking, or "packing-in," as it was called years ago. The site of your mountain home might be within reach of trails and routes that backpackers use. Try to select a spot that is removed from constant traffic of this sort. What only recently was a pristine woodland may quickly become an ecological nightmare of cigarette wrappers and beer cans.

In some localities of the West, in areas controlled by city, state, or federal agencies, you may be able to lease land from the government upon which to erect a home. In that case, you will have to abide by the rules and regulations set up by the controlling agency. Because of these regulations, you have the advantage of knowing that no one will come in with bulldozers and build a ten-story condominium next to you one day.

SKI AND SNOW

If life in the mountains is rugged, life in the ski and snow area is even more so. Not only must a second home in the ski area be built snug and tight, but it must also be structurally resistant to accumulations of snow and ice and the buffeting of wind, sleet, and hail, and it must be placed out of danger of avalanches, landslides, and flooding.

Although some ski homes are built right into the mountains, most of them are not. The site that is most favored is one that is protected, safe, and, of course, close to a good ski run. You have a great deal of latitude in the type of site you can select: on a mountain slope, in a valley, or on flat meadowland.

One point should be especially considered. Skiing is a group sport activity rather than a solitary sport. The ski-and-snow home must be large enough to accommodate guests and do so during extremely rugged weather. The site also

The pitched roof will shed snow and prevent pile-up of ice. Hand-split resewn shakes provide natural texture for structure's exterior.

must have easy access to it in order to accommodate host and guests during a time of the year when weather conditions are generally foul and driving is dangerous.

Numerous designs are available for ski-and-snow homes, many of them based on the extremely viable A-frame or Swiss chalet model. The basic A-frame structure is perfect for snow country; the shape of the roof sheds snow as soon as it falls, and the triangular shape resists the pressure of the most savage wind and rain. The A-frame takes up a good deal more ground area than an ordinary box-shaped structure; think of that when you select your site.

The ski-and-snow home should have a large guest potential; it should be snug and tight to retain heat; it should have a good furnace; it should be able to sustain men and women who are outdoors much of the time but who want comfort and safety when they are inside. The site you choose must be able to support such a house.

SELECTION OF SITE

No matter what kind of recreational area you may want to settle in, and no matter what type of second home you plan to build, you should pay attention to some very general considerations that have to do with selection of the site of the second home.

Essentially, they are: proximity, isolation versus community living, financing, accessibility, utilities, security, drainage, erosion, zoning laws, construction costs, community living, flora and fauna, and weather.

Proximity. Once you have decided on the general geographical area in which you want to build, you must select a specific place in that area fairly close to your first home. Too long a drive to your second home will tire you out so much that you cannot enjoy yourself when you finally get to your leisure home.

Most owners of second houses have found that any trip over two hours is a tiring one. A trip that takes three hours and more is much too exhausting and is to be avoided if possible.

Your best bet is to select a site that takes only an hour to reach. You can manage a site that takes two hours to reach, but you had better pass up a site that takes three hours or more to reach, after you have left the heavy, slow-moving city traffic.

In the old days, when vacation homes were used only in summer, they could be located at a great distance. The entire family packed up once, drove there, and stayed until the end of the season. Nowadays, however, with the increased use of automobiles on improved road systems, most people tend to use their second homes the year round, on weekends, and whenever they have a chance to get away from the work grind.

Isolation Versus Community Living. Your main purpose in owning a second home may be to get as far away as possible from the hustle and bustle of the city—to live, in effect, the life of a hermit. This may be an understandable desire in view of the fast, nerve-racking pace of modern life, but you should think twice about living in complete isolation.

People through the ages have tended to settle in groups rather than singly. There are advantages to living alone, but there are more advantages to living together and sharing certain responsibilities.

Some of the popular and successful vacation and leisure communities today stress communal living, with the houses grouped together for the residents' mutual benefit.

Financing. By far the most important advantage of living in a group-oriented leisure community is the matter of financing construction work on your second home. Unless you are independently wealthy and can raise about twenty thousand dollars in cash immediately, you must think hard about how you are going to finance your dream home.

The use of sliding glass doors and many windows brings light into the house at all times, with the open boxed beam ceiling providing a free-flowing and airy feeling.

In a community that is being developed for more than one family, you will find that banking and financing institutions are already in the picture and waiting to serve you.

A bank is always much more willing to advance money to twenty families for twenty second homes than it is to advance money to one family for a single second home. And not only will the lending institution be more willing to underwrite your construction project, but the terms will be nominal and easier for you to meet.

Accessibility. You may select one of the most beautiful spots in America on the side of a hill where the view of the mountains, lakes, and valleys is breathtaking, but you may have inadvertently chosen a spot that you could never get to without spending thousands of dollars to build an access road.

Or perhaps you may select the one site in an area to which it is impossible to drive because of a right-of-way or other legal obstacles. For, if someone owns the strip of land between your proposed site and the main public road, you simply cannot get through his land to yours.

Or perhaps you want to build on a lakefront site that is high protected land; yet the only access to your proposed property goes through a swamp that would demand the construction of an expensive bridge.

Because it is such an extremely important factor, accessibility should be investigated thoroughly before you make any arrangements to buy a site. Since accessibility is a built-in part of a community development, you do not have to worry about roadways and rights-of-way.

Utilities. Water, electric power, and sewage disposal are as necessary to consider in a second home as they are in a first.

The accessibility to water is most important in the second home. Usually, in most sections of the country, you can sink a well and pump in water if you do not have it at hand. However, there are areas close to lakes where water is not always available, and there are remote dry areas where water is not available at all. To bring it in from outside sources can cost a great deal of money; you can ill afford to build in an area without water.

You must find out the low and high marks of the underground water table, that is, the level under the surface of the earth where water usually lies. It will sink during the summer months as moisture drains off or dries up, and it will rise during the fall rains and the spring thaw. A knowledge of the water table will tell you how deep your well must be sunk in order to reach water for the dry period of the year.

Any water you plan to use should be tested for pollutants at the nearest county or state department of health. Some hidden elements may be dirtying the water you intend to use. It is a nasty shock to find that water which looks clear is in reality poisonous and unusable.

To obviate the problem of water, you can build in a community that has a water supply available to each member.

Modern living demands electric power to a degree unimagined even fifty years ago. The old days of a cabin in the woods lighted by a kerosine lamp and heated by a Franklin stove is a thing of the past, unhappily so, perhaps.

Electricity, water, and sewage disposal are necessities in today's vacation house. Without utilities you cannot run a kitchen such as this one.

Nevertheless, your second home should be built near some source of electric power. If you cannot find an available supply, you must consider the cost of running a gasoline-powered generator to power the house. In a second-home community, electric power is usually provided along with water as part of the package.

The hermit of old could completely ignore the problem of sewage and waste disposal. He could bury his tin cans underground and let the jackals and coyotes feast on his garbage.

Nowadays, pollution of the environment is one of the most important considerations for the occupants of any remote area. If you build your own second home on an isolated site, you must not only provide for a septic tank, but you must also find a place to bury your garbage and destroy your refuse without polluting the atmosphere.

In areas that are still pristine, the problem becomes one of major proportions. Sewage dis-

posal is also a high-priority consideration for any community; group living causes the problem and must solve it.

Security. A major consideration for almost anyone with a house in an isolated area is that of security. With no local police force on duty twenty-four hours a day, a closed second home becomes a prime target for roving bands of thieves who make a business of breaking in and removing anything easily disposable. In some cases entire cabins have been stolen. They were simply loaded onto a flatbed and hauled away!

Protection from thieves is no laughing matter. If you live in a community development with people all around you, the security problem will be handled by experienced individuals hired by the community for that very purpose. If you live off by yourself—look out!

Drainage. No matter where you want to build a second home, you must consider a most important point: drainage.

Even in a year-round house, drainage can become a fantastically expensive and irritating problem, causing flooded cellars, eroding lawns, muddy driveways, and sinking foundations.

Locating a house on high ground is always an advantage to any homeowner. Land located on the bottom of a slope or on flat land can be subject to flooding because of bad or sluggish drainage. Be sure that the site you select has adequate drainage and will not become the bottom of a flood basin.

Erosion. The problem of erosion goes hand in hand with the problem of drainage.

Even the highest part of a hill may slowly erode if constantly attacked by rain or running water. High ground is preferred ground, but if there is any danger of its eroding, do not select it for a building site.

It is possible to inspect any piece of terrain to judge if it is erosion-prone. If you see furrows making deep inroads into soil that is not adequately overgrown with grass or covered by weeds, brush or trees, you can be sure that the first rains will tear away the dirt and send it sliding downward.

You should also test high ground for rock faults and hidden crevasses. Such "faults" can cause the entire slope to slide at the first heavy rain or geologic disturbance, like an earth tremor.

Zoning Laws. A second home should be situated where there is peace and quiet. For this reason, you should make sure that the pristine stillness you observe when you first visit the site will not be ruined on Memorial Day by the squalling shrieks of thousands of small-fry on outings, which could continue all through summer.

Zoning is the best kind of protection available to you as a potential buyer of real estate. Zoning laws can be bent, however, if the man wanting to do the bending has sufficient money and political clout. It is a wise idea to investigate the area carefully to see what is happening in the real estate market—and on the political front.

If the site you want is located in the middle of valuable mining or oil land that might make a fortune for the owners—look out! Likewise, if the same land looks good for a big commercial amusement park or huge motel, stay away.

Subscribe to the local newspaper to find out which developer is in control of things and which local politician is the mover who makes things go in the community. Then see if he has your interests at heart.

If the political situation seems stable, you will probably be safe from zoning shenanigans. Nevertheless, zoning problems exist wherever there is undeveloped land that can be manipulated to bring in fast easy money for its owners. Check the zoning laws carefully in the county clerk's office to see if they are foolproof—or only *look* foolproof.

Irregular-shaped stones gathered just outside this house were formed into a handsome fireplace.

Construction Costs. The cost of building materials varies radically from place to place, as does the cost of labor. If you are going to perform all the construction tasks on your second home yourself, you will not be subject to the problem of labor costs, but you will have to consider material costs.

In a wooded area, you can sometimes use native lumber where it is found in its growing state. Usually, however, you will have to depend on wood that has been milled to some degree. If stone is handy, you can always use that for foundations, for fireplaces, and for some walls, but only if you are a skilled mason.

Materials and construction costs zoom when you are forced to carry materials into an area that is difficult to reach with heavy equipment. If you need a great deal of excavation work or must clear a lot of timber or brush from the property, you will have to expect appropriately higher construction costs.

If you have to provide an access road to your property, you must expect to pay plenty, and though some access roads are relatively simple to build, others are very difficult. If a bridge needs to be put up, the cost will be very high.

You must also consider that construction costs will be higher if the house must withstand excessive loads of snow and ice in the winter months.

Never forget that you must perform all construction in accordance with local building codes and labor practices.

Community Living. The preceding points have all illustrated to some degree the advantage of buying property and erecting a second home in a community development composed of similar houses.

Financing, accessibility, utilities, security, drainage, erosion, zoning, and construction costs all become factors in the construction of your second home. The advantage in these instances of community development is obvious; whether or not it outweighs your own personal prejudgments as to the advantage of isolation over community life is a decision you yourself will have to make.

Flora and Fauna. There are certain questions that might come up concerning plants and animals living on the building site you want to use.

As for the trees on the site, try to imagine how they will affect your daily life. They should let the wind move around the house to provide essential ventilation of air, yet they should not let in too much destructive wind. They should give adequate shade, yet not cut out needed light.

As for the shrubs and smaller growth on the property, you should remove for your own protection accumulations of poisonous plants like poison oak, poison ivy, ragweed, poison sumac, and the like. If there are certain trees or shrubs that cause allergies in members of your family, you will have to get rid of them.

No less important than the vegetation present is the wild life living on the property or nearby. If you plan to spend your leisure time fishing, you should make sure that the lake or stream or ocean sustains enough fish for your recreational purposes. If you plan to hunt small game, such as rabbits, squirrels, or waterfowl, you should find out if there is enough of it about.

On the other hand, you will want to avoid annoying pests like bears, rats, porcupines, skunks, mice, and snakes. Insects such as mosquitoes, gnats, yellow jackets, and ants are particularly irritating and should be avoided or controlled.

Weather. Variations in weather can be a very important consideration to the prospective purchaser of property for a second home. In fact, weather conditions can vary from one place to another within very short distances.

Generally speaking, mountain winds blow up-canyon during the day and downcanyon during the night; hot or heating air rises and cold or cooling air sinks. Sea winds blow away from the sea during the day and toward the sea during the night.

It is best to select a site away from a "wind gap." You will know a wind gap exists if you see trees and other vegetation that lean sideways, or if there is a sudden bare spot in a lot of natural growth.

Remember that cold air, because it is heavier than warm air, tends to settle in pockets or depressions in the terrain. Mountain meadows that are comfortable during the daytime can be extremely cold at night unless they are open to circulating air.

Weather also differs from season to season. A place with delightful spring weather may become a hot desert oven in the summer. Winter may bring snow enough to keep you away from an otherwise pleasant woodland site, and certain beaches may be afflicted with fogs all during the summer months.

HOW TO BUY PROPERTY

There are a number of ways to proceed with shopping for real estate once you have decided upon where you want to build.

Probably the most logical and the simplest is to put yourself in the hands of a real estate agent. Be sure he is a reputable man—that is, he belongs to the local real estate board or to the National Association of Real Estate Boards (NAREB). Tell him what you are looking for, and stress the limits of your financial means. Then let him get in touch with you when he finds something he thinks you will like.

Another simple way is to put an advertisement in the newspaper printed in the general area you have selected. You may find that real estate agents or individual sellers will contact you. Either way, you are apt to come up with something.

A third way, which is rather hit-or-miss, is to take a trip through the general area in which you want to settle. If there are farm houses or cabins located there, stop to chat with the owners. You may find that the person you talk to is about to pull up stakes for another part of the country, or that as a property owner he is willing to sell you a piece of his land for a fair price.

And you can always subscribe to the newspaper published in the community and keep a close check on the real estate ads. In that way you can at the same time also familiarize yourself with the problems and advantages of the community.

Chapter 2

PLYWOOD CONSTRUCTION

BETWEEN the dream of a second home and its completion lie a great many considerations and decisions that you must make. Aside from aesthetic values and available locations, the most important of these is the over-all cost of the project.

Without exception, everyone wants a place just a bit better than he can afford. The final price must be a compromise between what you would really like and what you are able to pay.

Although building materials cost a great deal everywhere, the main financial consideration in any type of construction today is labor. You can realize considerable savings by doing part or all of the work yourself. Perhaps you are an expert carpenter and craftsman; in that case, you can put up the entire structure yourself. Or perhaps you are eager but inexperienced, and you want to do as much as possible of the job yourself not only to cut costs but to have the fulfillment of accomplishment. Or perhaps you are lazy, rich, both, and want someone else to shoulder the entire burden and put your house up for you.

Between the least expensive kind of building, where you do it all yourself and only pay out money for materials, to the most expensive kind, where you hire an architect and contractor, there are several gradations. At each gradation you can look at cabin plans and cabin packages prepared for your benefit.

But before you go off half-cocked and try to build a cabin out of sawed-down trees all by yourself or you make up your mind to put yourself entirely in the hands of an architect and contractor, you should know exactly what kind of construction packages are open to you at the present time.

A DO-IT-YOURSELF PLAN

The least expensive and most difficult type of construction is that which you do all by yourself. You can always draw your own plan for a house, but unless you are an architect of some experience, it is not a particularly good idea in these days of zoning laws, building codes, insurance considerations, and so on.

It is a wise idea instead to put yourself in the hands of people who have made a long study of vacation homes and have developed plans for them that have been put to the acid test already.

The American Plywood Association is a group

of over forty-nine lumber companies that manufacture plywood paneling and siding. Among the largest represented by American Plywood are Weyerhaeuser Company, U. S. Plywood, Georgia-Pacific Corporation, Boise Cascade Corporation, and The Pacific Lumber Company.

All paneling produced by companies belonging to APA adhere to standards of quality set up by the Association; these standards are explained later in this chapter. Distribution varies from area to area in the United States. You may find your supplier stocked with Georgia-Pacific; or he may sell you Birmingham Forest Products. Both belong to APA; the quality of each piece can be counted on to be carefully graded for your use.

Because it is in the business of encouraging the use of plywood, the American Plywood Association has developed a number of excellent plans featuring the use of plywood in vacation cabins and year-round second homes, six of which appear in this chapter.

Each of these plans presents an imaginative, practical, and different approach to the cabin or second home, and they are designed for the amateur who wants to save money as well as construct a good leisure home.

COST CONSIDERATIONS

Cost is one of the most important considerations in construction, but it is impossible to quote accurate prices in a book of this kind written for use in all fifty states.

Materials differ from state to state—indeed, from mile to mile within each state. So do labor costs. For that reason, you will have to use a rather flexible rule of thumb in order to calculate the final cost of the cabins and houses featured here.

Generally speaking, architects and contractors predicate final cost on a square-foot basis. That is, if a cabin is 12 by 15 feet in size, it has an area of 180 square feet.

Most plywood construction of this type can be brought in—that is, completed—at a cost of from $14 to $20 per square foot.

Thus a 12-by-15-foot cabin would cost from $2,520 to $3,600.

Cost factors shift considerably from day to day and from area to area. The above scale has been calculated for the type of second home described in this chapter. The total cost will simply be an approximation to the nearest thousand dollars, roughly speaking.

Later on, where more elaborate structures are considered, the cost factor may rise about $5 to $10 per square foot. It would not be outrageous to say that the cost factor in a more expensive vacation home would be $25 to $30 per square foot, depending on the materials and labor used.

The cost factor figure quoted, incidentally, includes electricity, plumbing, and utilities of all kinds, plus all interior finishing, such as paint, stain, or wallpaper.

By doing the labor yourself, you will probably save a little over 50 percent of the square-foot cost. In the above 12-by-15-foot cabin, figured $14-$20, you would save about $1,210-$1,800. Local price fluctuations regarding both materials and labor will throw this figure out of line, of course.

Because of the difficulty in quoting prices, most companies dealing in construction costs will not make a flat rate for a house applicable to all areas of the country. Neither can we. We can only approximate to the nearest thousand dollars.

THE PLYWOOD HOUSE

Modern building techniques have made the construction of a vacation home faster, easier, and better than it has ever been. Conventional material used in seasonal homes includes masonry walls made of stone found on the site, concrete or aggregate blocks, kiln-fired brick, adobe brick, logs cut on the site, crib construction of milled framing pieces, wood framework of all kinds, and plywood.

Of all these, the type of material that is at once the most inexpensive, the quickest, and the most reliable construction material available to the amateur builder is plywood. In combination with masonry, concrete blocks, brick, logs, and other types of wood framework, plywood usually serves as the base even for the more complicated construction done by professionals.

It is a modern material that is strong, durable, and rigid; it withstands weather of all kinds quite successfully, can survive high winds, and has even come through earthquakes with reasonable success.

Because vacation cabins and leisure homes made of plywood are simple and can be erected with a minimum of skill and technical knowledge, plywood material is one of the most popular kinds of wood in use by amateur do-it-yourself builders today.

It is made up of an odd number of veneer sheets glued together, with the grains of the layers usually at right angles to one another. Because of this cross-ply lamination, plywood has strength across the grain as well as lengthwise along it.

With the wood grain of one veneer running in one direction and that of the next layer running at right angles to the first, plywood shrinks or swells less than an ordinary piece of wood does. Also, the impact of a blow is distributed over the entire face surface of the panel instead of being concentrated on one spot.

Because of the laminated structure of plywood, you can place nails and screws in it with less chance of splitting the wood. Plywood is much easier to work with because of its resistance to chipping and breaking.

Once in place, plywood has excellent insulating qualities. It can also weather the elements well and is known as a most durable construction material.

Sizes of Panels. Plywood is manufactured in panel modules of 4 by 8 feet, 4 by 10 feet, and 4 by 12 feet. It also comes in other sizes, but these are the most common. The 4-by-8 panel is by far the most popular of the three sizes.

Because in home construction the ceiling is usually designed to hang eight feet from the floor, the 4-by-8-foot panel can be placed upright along each wall without any cutting or fitting. And because most upright framing timbers in home construction, called "studs" are placed 16 or 24 inches "on center"—that is, with the centers exactly 16 or 24 inches apart—the 48-inch width easily accommodates three studs spaced 16 inches apart or two studs spaced 24 inches apart without any cutting of the panel.

Plywood comes in various thicknesses, starting with 1/4 inch and going through 3/8 inch, 1/2 inch, 3/4 inch, and 1 inch, with other variations available.

The plans that follow have been developed to utilize different kinds of plywood to their greatest potential, and they have been designed for the amateur do-it-yourselfer to help him save money and enable him to get the best possible second home for his money.

THREE-STAGER

The Three-Stager is a very simple vacation unit that has been designed with economy and practicality in mind. It can be constructed on a shoestring. As soon as you have finished one third of the house, you can use this first stage as a livable cabin.

A small outlay of money will start construction. As soon as you have some more to spend, you can add on the second stage, and finally finish the third stage at your leisure.

The Three-Stager has been designed with an eye to modern architectural concepts and to take advantage of the informal "back-to-nature" atmosphere of lake, seashore, or trout stream.

Stage One consists of almost 300 square feet of living space in a very compact area, providing kitchenette, bath, and living/sleeping area. The cabin fulfills all the needs of the weekend carpenter or handyman.

The details of the plan have been worked out

to make use of full-size 4-by-8 sheets of plywood as much as possible throughout the house, minimizing excess cutting and wastage in construction.

The foundation has been engineered for post-and-beam construction to simplify erection and to make it applicable to uneven, soggy, or rocky ground.

The deck has been designed for a lot of outdoor living. Actually, it will almost double the usable area of the vacation house in good weather. In Stage Two, of course, the deck actually becomes the floor of half of the second unit.

Stage One is not Howard Hughes's idea of a hunting lodge, but it can serve for an ordinary family—with kitchen, bath, and bedroom facilities small but usable.

Stage Two will give you plenty of space to move around in. The deck of Stage One becomes the living room of Stage Two, and another 16-foot deck then extends out from the living room for even more deck space than was provided in Stage One.

A window wall overlooking the new deck and the addition of a fireplace adds comfort and elegance to your vacation hideaway. There are three clerestory windows at the side that provide a modern touch.

Stage Two gives you 576 square feet of living area, as against 288 for Stage One. Stage Three provides for 864 square feet of living area, so that by the time you have finished the third and final stage, you will have a full-scale three-bedroom vacation retreat.

If you want to open the original sleeping/living room to the service unit, you can remove

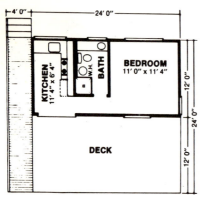
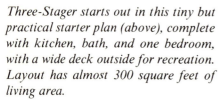
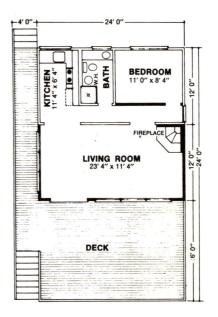

Three-Stager starts out in this tiny but practical starter plan (above), complete with kitchen, bath, and one bedroom, with a wide deck outside for recreation. Layout has almost 300 square feet of living area.

Second step is to finish off Stage Two (opposite right), which gives you a total of almost 600 square feet of living area—just about twice Stage One. A large living room is added on to the basic plan of Stage One.

1790588
THREE-STAGER

A three-bedroom house (above), emerges from the temporary dwellings constructed in Stage One and Two. Plan uses plywood modules to simplify construction and to cut costs.

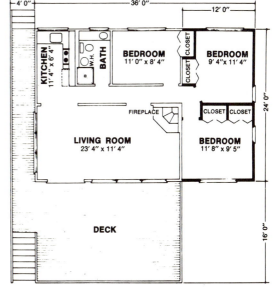

Interior shows finished Three-Stager completely furnished for informal living. Interior paneling is prefinished and requires minimum maintenance.

one nonbearing partition and add on more. The plans for the construction of the Three-Stager include details for all three stages, along with an alternate perimeter foundation if you need it to abide by building restrictions.

As a finished vacation home, the Three-Stager will give you a large living area, a kitchen, a bath, three bedrooms, and a wide expanse of decking in front and along the side.

For the amateur builder, with the help of a neighbor or friend, the construction time on the Three-Stager should not take more than two weeks for Stage One, not including plumbing and electrical work; about two weeks for Stage Two; and two weeks more for Stage Three.

The 228 square feet of Stage One should cost about $16 per square foot; the 576 square feet of Stage Two (which includes Stage One) should cost about $15 per square foot; and the 864 square feet of Stage Three (which includes Stages One and Two) should cost about $14 per square foot.

That would bring the total cost of all three stages to approximately $12,096 for the finished Three-Stager.

DOUBLE-CLUSTER CABIN

The design of the Double-Cluster Cabin consists basically of two large plywood building blocks connected with a roofed-in breezeway.

But each half of this vacation home has been designed with alternate floor plans to enable you to choose from several different concepts.

Each building module in the accompanying floor plan is exactly the same size. The interior living areas are simply arranged to allow for a choice of room arrangements, different budgets, and a variety of building sites.

Unit A, the basic living room/kitchen/bath unit, has been designed as the basic starter unit, just like Stage One of the Three-Stager discussed previously. The 16-by-24-foot living area is organized to give you everything you need for temporary quarters. Included are kitchen, bath, dining space, a place for daybed and bunks, and even a fireplace. You can live here while you are working on the second half.

Unit B—an alternate to Unit A—is also a starter unit, but there is no bathroom; the idea is to include the bath in the second half of the house. Leaving out the bath gives you a great deal more interior living area for dining and moving about.

Unit C is the first of two possible "second half" cluster plans. It has two or three bedrooms, a

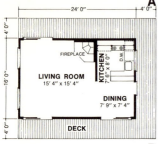

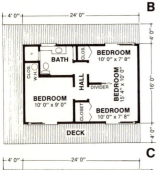

full bathroom, and large adjoining storage spaces.

The number of bedrooms is optional and can be changed by the use of a "divider," or movable screen, that permits you to shift one end of the living area into smaller and more private sectors. If the bath has been included in the starter half of the house, you can use that area for a second bath, or for another bedroom or storage room.

Unit D, an alternate to Unit C, shows a different type of bedroom arrangement. The main feature here is the generous walk-in wardrobe closet assigned to each bedroom. Both bedrooms are 11 feet 6 inches by 9 feet and have plenty of wall space for furniture. A full bathroom between the wardrobes serves both bedrooms.

Each of these four clusters contains 384 square feet of living area.

The illustration shows the simple two-block cluster plan, using Unit A and Unit D described above, to complete the Double-Cluster Cabin.

The completed vacation home is planned as a post-and-beam elevated structure so that the foundation can be adapted with ease to rough and uneven building sites.

The two units are combined under a roof that forms a breezeway between the two blocks. This type of home has been proved to be quite practical in many different test situations.

Each plan is designed with 4-by-8 plywood modules in mind. The cost of construction is kept low because of minimum wastage from cutting and shaping.

The secret of Double-Cluster Cabin—and Triple-Cluster, too—lies in the block-type modules shown above. Of the four modules shown, the first two—A and B—can be used as a basic living-room module, the second two—C and D—for a basic bedroom module.

DOUBLE-CLUSTER CABIN

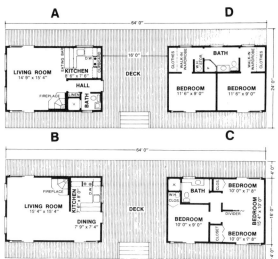

One living-room module and one bedroom module have been combined into a Double-Cluster Cabin (above). The alternate floor plans show two of four possibilities for combining living-room and bedroom modules into separate vacation houses. Interior below shows living-room module of the Double-Cluster unit.

The Double-Cluster combination gives you two baths, two bedrooms, with space for a fold-out bed in the basic unit, and kitchen and dining area.

You should be able to bring in the entire job of 768 square feet for about $16 per square foot in something over six weeks. The time-consuming work—the finishing-off—can come later, of course.

Total cost for the job would be about $12,288.

TRIPLE-THREAT CLUSTER CABIN

Now look at the Triple-Threat Cluster Cabin and see if you can figure out how it is put together.

Right!

Your old friend Unit B, from the Double-Cluster Cabin, has been placed in the front, with Unit D attached to it by breezeway. And Unit C has been turned sideways and attached at the rear.

Ingenious?

Unit B has been used along with C and D to achieve a triple-threat design that will take full advantage of a great view.

Notice how the living room and dining areas and two of the bedrooms face in this "best view" direction. Also, you can see that the steps from the large deck space connect with the waterfront, the trout stream, or other main point of interest in the vacation site.

From a study of the Double-Cluster Cabin and the Triple-Threat Cluster Cabin, you will see that the base modules can be put together in a variety of ways. In fact, with alterations in basic deck

In this Triple-Module Cabin, living-room Unit B from page 38 and bedroom Units C and D have been combined in a slightly different fashion, creating a brand-new design for vacation home.

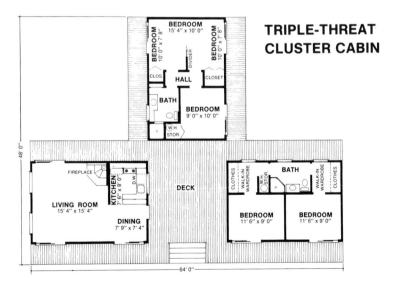

TRIPLE-THREAT CLUSTER CABIN

space and the addition of other units, the choices of floor plans are almost limitless.

The raised-pole type of foundation has been shown in both these units, but plans for these houses come complete with details for a conventional perimeter-type foundation if it is required by building codes in areas near population centers.

The Triple-Threat will take about ten weeks to put up, with the 1,152 square feet of living space costing about $16 per square foot. The total for the whole job should be about $18,432.

DOUBLE-DECK A-FRAME

The A-frame is one of the most intriguing and popular of all vacation-home designs ever invented. Man has been putting up A-frame dwellings ever since he came out of the cave,

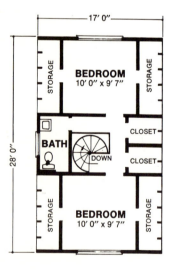
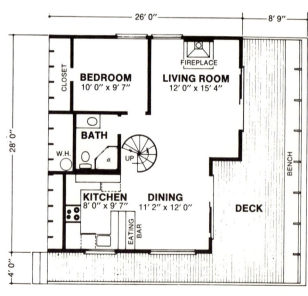

DOUBLE-DECK A-FRAME

Modified A-frame has plenty of room upstairs and downstairs, with a spiral staircase the focal point of the living room.

such as the teepee, the army tent, the wickiup.

Today the A has come back in strength for use in the woods and even by the sea. The triangular shape holds its rigidity under the most destructive forces of nature. The sloped roof sheds water beautifully and resists accumulations of snow or ice that might crush any other structure of similar size.

The Double-Deck A-Frame shown here has the advantage of a second story for undisturbed sleeping away from the living quarters below.

Structurally, this A rests on oversized beams supported by concrete pilings. Plywood panels, properly edge-butted and nailed, give the rigidity needed for this kind of building.

Kitchen, bath, living room, bedroom, and dining area are located on the first floor. Two roomy dormitory-type bedrooms are situated on the floor above, with connecting bath and large closet storage space for both bedrooms.

The upper level is reached by the focal point of the interior design: a beautiful circular stairway that does not take up needed living space.

The main floor plan permits easy traffic flow through the living room, dining area, kitchen, and master bedroom. In addition a spacious deck runs the width of the dwelling on one side and extends along the side next to the kitchen/dining area.

There is a total of 1,156 square feet of living space in this Double-Deck A-Frame, enough for a very good weekend party—and you will never have to worry about anyone knocking the walls down.

The skeleton of this structure is formed by two frames consisting of heavy end beams joined at the top by conventional additional roof surfacing.

The A can be put up in about six weeks. The first 680 square feet—the lower floor—will cost about $15 per square foot. The next 476 square feet—the upper—will cost about $8 per square foot.

That brings the total to about $14,008.

RETIREMENT HAVEN

If you have been dreaming of a small, economical vacation hideaway that will be sufficiently comfortable for a permanent retirement home later on, then take a look at this compact little house.

The practical design gives you a great deal of comfort and the convenience of a much bigger house without the extra cost of building and maintaining it. It is also designed for a view from both front and back.

At the front, three sliding glass doors open out onto a big family deck that is ideal for outdoor living most of the year in warm and moderate climates.

At the back, windows look out not only from the living room and kitchen, but also from the rear bedroom. Well-planned skylights open up the house visually on overcast or depressing days.

The interior is planned to utilize every square foot of space, with bedrooms as big or even bigger than you sometimes find in a suburban house.

The dining area is big enough for a family reunion. And on weekends or at other times when the house may be bursting at the seams

Two floor plans are available for Retirement Haven. The variations involve the placement of the fireplace, and the difference in the number of bedrooms—two or three.

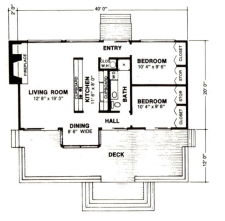
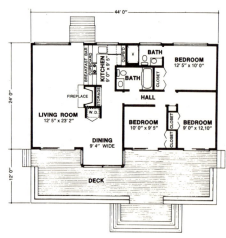

with people, the usual crowd problems are minimized by the provision of outside access to the deck from two of the bedrooms, plus another entry to the outdoors from the dining area.

There are two house sizes available in this design: the first, with 837 square feet of living area, has two bedrooms; the second, with 1096 square feet of living area, has three bedrooms. With its large, spacious areas, the second house can easily serve as a year-round dwelling.

The Retirement Haven has been planned for plywood construction throughout, not only to simplify the building job but to hold down costs.

You can use the money you save in choosing this house to buy yourself other retirement accessories—new fishing gear, perhaps or a new boat. Or, if you decide to do some of the work yourself, maybe you can even buy yourself a brand-new second car!

Approximately eight weeks should bring in the house. The smaller version, at 837 square feet, should cost about $14 per square foot—a total of $11,718. The larger version, at 1,096 square feet, should cost about $13 per square foot—a total of $14,248.

ROUNDHOUSE

Suppose you are trying to find the right house for the perfect vacation site which includes a panoramic view in front, a beautiful garden to the right, an untouched sparkling stream to the left, and a beautiful woods to the rear.

Once you get the house, which way should the structure face for the best view and the most artistic effect?

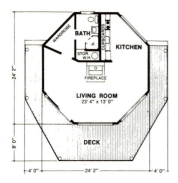

The answer to the question is a simple one: Build a house that looks out on all sides!

The Roundhouse is designed for exactly that purpose, and even though it is not round at all, but is an eight-sided structure, it resembles a roundhouse. And it is perfect for use on a site that has sensational view in every direction.

The Roundhouse pictured here comes in three sizes: 309 square feet, 482 square feet, and 695 square feet. No matter what size lot you have, you can find a Roundhouse plan to fit it.

The smallest size is planned for a living/sleeping/dining area with separate kitchen and bath divisions.

The middle size has a similar floor plan, but all the areas are enlarged.

The largest size has two different styles:

One shifts the floor plan slightly, adds a bedroom, and enlarges the living-room area. A fireplace or Franklin stove provides an excellent focal point.

The second style plan cuts back the general living area to provide for two bedrooms.

The house pictured here is the large-sized

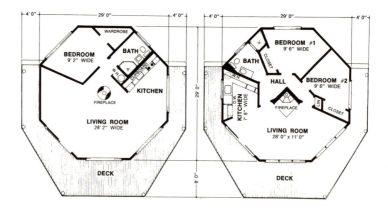

This Roundhouse comes in three sizes—309 square feet, 482 square feet, or 695 square feet—with a corresponding difference in price.

Roundhouse, containing 695 square feet of living area. Even though the actual area seems small in comparison with the larger houses pictured in this chapter, the Roundhouse gives you all the conveniences of a year-round residence, with a lot more added.

There are two spacious bedrooms, a 28-by-12 foot living room, a kitchen, and a bath. For relaxation outdoors, a post-and-beam deck extends around five sides of the house.

The interior in the photograph is finished with rough-sawn redwood plywood paneling and gold wall-to-wall carpeting. The ceiling is a sweeping, dramatic one, with purlins that radiate outward from a center compression ring.

In the center, a black iron fireplace encased in a background of used brick acts as the focal point of the interior. The rugged natural look of the cabin's exterior is attained by using hand-split shakes and rough-sawn fir plywood siding.

The heating in this particular house is provided by a forced-air electric heating unit, mounted under the crawl space and ducted to the rooms throughout the house.

The Roundhouse plan makes use of plywood to provide a solid base for a shake or shingle roof, and also to make floor construction easier.

You can use siding of rough-sawn plywood with a low-maintenance stain finish in a board-and-batten style as pictured, or you can use overlaid plywood painted in bright colors, which would be especially appropriate for a beach setting.

As for price, you can bring in the Roundhouse, small size, 309 square feet, for approximately $4,635, figuring the base cost as from $14 to $16 per square-foot finish price—including foundation, plumbing, electricity, and so on, exclusive of furnishings.

The middle-sized house, 482 square feet, figures at $7,230, and the giant-sized house, 695 square feet, at $10,425.

PLYWOOD SURFACES

Incidentally, these plans all make full use of plywood, not only for subfloors and underlayment, but on ceilings, and, most important, on interior and exterior wall surfaces.

There are dozens of different types of textured plywood siding available: board and batten, flat panel, wide-lapped, and so on. Likewise, many different "face" woods are available: cedar, redwood, Douglas fir, lauan (Philippine mahogany), southern pine—to mention only a few.

The same is true of prefinished interior plywood paneling. You can get it in many varieties and textures and finish the surface off yourself, or buy prefinished plywood paneling that is maintenance-free from the time you put it in place.

Chapter Ten shows some of the varieties of patterns and surfaces available in both exterior and interior plywood surfaces.

Plywood takes paint well, too. Chapter Eleven tells you how to paint both exterior and interior plywood surfaces for best results.

Do It Yourself—Or Not? The plans discussed here are all available from the American Plywood Association at the present time. They can be used as working drawings for the experienced do-it-yourselfer or for the professional contractor.

If you believe that you have enough professional skill, you can build each of these houses yourself, using the plans as guidelines.

If you are an amateur, you would do well to study the construction techniques discussed in Chapter Nine to see if you can or cannot master them. If you believe you can, go ahead yourself. If, however, you do not know enough about carpentry to do the job, you can hire a contractor or builder to put up the cabin's shell for you; then you can proceed to finish off the interior yourself.

Hiring a contractor is discussed in detail in Chapter Eight; the information there pertains not only to contractors, but to subcontractors as well—plumbers, electricians, and heating men.

Chapter 3

PRECUT CONSTRUCTION

DOING all the labor involved in the construction of a vacation house yourself is a complicated job, one for which you may have neither the aptitude nor the skill.

Yet you may be an amateur do-it-yourselfer competent enough to want to do *almost* everything, bypassing only the more meticulous operations of carpentry that are irksome and tedious even for the professional. If this is the case, the answer may be "precut" construction, designed especially for the amateur who wants to do as much of the work as he can but still construct a livable home.

THE "SHELL" OF THE HOUSE

Generally speaking, the materials prepared for assembly in a precut building package include only the lumber constituting the "shell" of a house.

In building parlance, the shell includes the floor, the walls, and the roof—those components of a structure that are first erected and which constitute the fundamental parts of any shelter.

The shell does not include the foundation. Because there are so many different kinds of terrain upon which a house can be built, the precut manufacturer makes no attempt to provide a foundation. That is for the buyer to provide. Usually the buyer hires a professional contractor to supply the foundation. Chapter Nine explains in more detail the several types of construction used for building foundations.

Nor does the shell include plumbing, wiring, heating, built-in furniture, finish surfaces, ceilings, interior wall surfaces, or other such items. Most interior partitions are also considered apart from the shell, although a load-bearing wall *is* part of it.

Thus the shell—floor, walls, and roof—will be supplied in a precut package unless otherwise specified by the manufacturer. The basic unit of any structure, the shell must be erected first before any finishing off can be started: wiring, plumbing, heating, and painting.

THE PRECUT PACKAGE

The precut home is prepared with several important considerations in mind.

Of the three main components of carpentry work—measuring, shaping, and fitting—the first two are by far the most painstaking and difficult to perform.

1. *Measuring* involves meticulous marking, paying particular attention to plans, and understanding exactly what the written directions put there by the architect mean.

2. *Shaping* involves careful sawing, filing, and planing to make the proper joint for a tight fit. Even a professional carpenter may waste pieces of lumber by making a sloppy cut.

3. *Fitting*, however—nailing together, screwing, bolting, or gluing—takes the least skill and craftsmanship of the three. It is in *fitting* that the amateur can shine.

And so, with these considerations in mind, the precut vacation-home "package" was developed to provide all the shell parts of a house cut and made ready to fit.

With lumber measured and shaped in a factory under controlled conditions by means of precision equipment in the hands of skilled craftsmen, any amateur do-it-yourselfer can reduce building time to a third, or possibly even to a quarter, of what a professional would take to erect the structure using conventional on-site building methods.

So, for just a bit more money than you would spend on the raw materials, you can purchase a "package" of precut materials out of which you can assemble a cabin or second home with very little difficulty and no professional skill or background.

A precut vacation-home package will supply you with every piece of lumber, precut to size and shape, to constitute the shell of a vacation home of a particular design, shape, and size.

ADVANTAGES OF PRECUT

There are six primary advantages to precut construction:

1. *Precut saves money.* A precut package can save you a great deal of money in bypassing the high hourly wage rates of carpenters and painters who would have to be hired if you were going to use professionals to build the entire job at the vacation site.

2. *Precut saves time.* In general, a precut package saves construction time on the site, because all preliminary measuring and shaping has been done beforehand, with only minor fitting left to be done on the location. In most precut packages, certain difficult joints are prefabricated—that is, shaped *and* assembled—at the factory to save you time and trouble on the building site.

3. *Precut saves waste.* Because each piece of wood is precut, you do not have to pay for "approximate" amounts of material, only to find later on that hundreds of pounds of valuable scrap lumber are left lying around the site after the house is finished.

4. *Precut saves freight.* Lumber in a precut package is usually kiln-dried to cure the wood beforehand, that is, to reduce the amount of moisture in green wood to prevent shrinking, twisting, and warping after it is in place. The reduced weight of the demoisturized wood after curing also cuts down on freight costs.

5. *Precut guarantees a tight fit.* Each piece of lumber in a precut structure is shaped under optimum factory conditions to the correct size. Because of accurate preshaping, you can be sure the house will be tight-fitting and without leaks.

6. *Precut guarantees a tested design.* Precut packaging gives you a professional design and at least some pretesting of the finished product. Because the design has been carefully developed and used elsewhere, you will be sure to get a final house that will have been proved out as to livability and durability.

COMPONENTS OF PRECUT PACKAGE

A precut vacation home "package" consists of bundles of construction materials delivered to the building site along with tools to fit them together and a book of instructions that tell you exactly which board to nail to which other board in a detailed step-by-step manual. A blueprint and a set of elevations are also included.

Each piece of wood comes in a packet with a number of other pieces related to it, with each bundle marked clearly, and each piece of lumber in it numbered. All you have to do is refer to the book, select the piece of lumber in question, and fasten it to the other piece designated in the instruction manual.

Lumber is supplied not only cut to size and shape, but with predrilled holes for bolts and screws where necessary.

Incidentally, the individual bundles are usually broken down to a size that can be carried by two people through terrain that is impassable in a car.

A good precut kit is designed to be erected by two or three people who have no prior building skills. However, any precut kit can be taken in hand by professionals and put up that much faster.

The typical precut package includes the following:

1. Four or five sets of plans
2. A set of erection drawings, or elevations, showing how the finished shell looks
3. An erection manual, telling you exactly how to go about assembling the components
4. A set of specifications for the finished house
5. A complete materials list
6. All tools necessary to assemble a weather-tight structure
7. Interior doors
8. Locks for doors and windows
9. Windows
10. Rough hardware
11. Roofing materials
12. Subflooring
13. Milled material
14. Interior and exterior trim
15. Decking where required
16. Nails, screws, and bolts

The typical precut package does *not* include plumbing, heating, electric wiring, lighting fixtures, electric appliances, foundation materials, cabinets, septic tank, and labor.

HOW MANY MAN-HOURS?

By following carefully the erection manual provided with a typical vacation-home package, a two-man crew can put up a 1,000-square-foot shell in a week or so, a three-man crew, in four or five working days.

The completed home takes longer, because you have to wait for subcontractors—plumbers, electricians and heating contractors—and, in some areas, building inspectors as well.

What can speed up construction is a thorough knowledge and understanding of each step described in the erection manual that comes with the material. Understanding is really the single most important ingredient required to turn in a fast, workmanlike job.

If you have at least one man in the team who is experienced in carpentry, your job will go that much faster. He will know how to read plans and handle construction materials effectively, without wasting time with the amateur's first bumbling efforts.

If you are close to a metropolitan area where supplies for foundation materials and subcontractors are readily available, you will find the job takes much less time.

WHEN TO BUILD

If you choose to build a vacation home in the winter, when snow is falling or heavy rains are inundating the area, you will experience delays and other difficulties.

It is a good idea to order your precut home immediately *after* the peak of the building season, but before the heavy freeze; or you can order it in the early spring *before* the building surge. At these off-peak periods, you have the best chance to get quick delivery on materials and to obtain skilled help for subcontracting.

EXPANDABLE DESIGNS

Many precut vacation-home packages are designed in such a way that they can be added to after the first unit is finished. However, because of the careful cutting and shaping of all material, you should use the manufacturer's suggested design in adding on other rooms to the original unit.

If you want to make certain changes in a predesigned floor plan, be sure to inform the manufacturer before he begins work on the parts. Certain plan shifts will cost money, others may not. Most manufacturers have plans available for adding on rooms, expanding existing facilities, or changing the shape of the structure.

If you do not like the plans a manufacturer has, you can always have him design your house for you as a custom job. Such an architectural assignment will probably cost several hundred dollars.

A precut house can be erected on a slab foundation, on a basement excavation, on a conventional foundation, on pilings, on a sloping lot, or on rocky soil.

UNIT ONE

As an example of a completely precut vacation cabin designed especially for the amateur to put up himself, let's take a design called Unit One, manufactured and offered by Shelter Kit Incorporated.

A photograph of Unit One completed shows the basic simplicity of the model. As constructed, it is a weathertight, uninsulated shell habitable in the package form offered.

It is designed with a 12-by-12-foot main room that has a 9-by-12-foot porch, or deck, attached to the front. The roof slopes to afford a 9-foot

height at the front, with a 7-foot 8-inch height at the rear. The 9-foot height gives you a sense of space inside, and the wide front doorway accentuates that feeling.

The cabin is designed for electric baseboard heat. With the addition of heaters, and with the addition of insulation, interior finish, and plumbing, the small unit can be made into a comfortable year-round house. However, if you choose not to use it all year round, you can install a wood-burning stove to provide for adequate summertime heat.

An elevation of the cabin shows the measurements in profile, the floor plan the simplicity of the design. Note that there are two sliding windows at the rear of the cabin, and sliding glass doors at the front of the main room.

Unit One, which is actually a shell, rather than a finished cabin, can be put up by two men who are amateurs at carpentry. Precut and predrilled material save money and time.

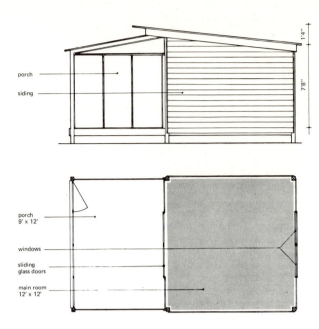

The basic shell of the cabin, exclusive of the foundation, consists of precut and predrilled wood timbers bolted together by means of aluminum angles and brackets to form a rigid, self-supporting structure. To this you nail flooring, siding, and roofing.

With good weather and proper care, two men in reasonably good health who have some skill should complete the shell-type cabin in four days.

Camping Out in Unit One. The smallest module of Unit One—the 12-by-12-foot structure—can serve adequately as a comfortable space for two people in a rough "camping out" situation. You can build in bunks with storage space beneath them, shelves, and a drop table. A small wood-burning stove will give enough heat in the uninsulated shell even for 20 degree Fahrenheit temperatures.

For cooking, use a propane stove. For furniture, use folding director chairs and inexpensive rough-hewn tables. The porch is large enough to accommodate two beds in warm weather.

The plan opposite shows you how to utilize the available space for a very snug camp.

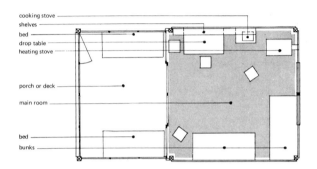

Expansion Plans. Unit One has been designed with an eye to expansion from the modular structure to a house twice as big, or even three or four times as big. You simply remove the exterior wall on one or both sides of the house and bolt on another module. In this way, you can add on partitions—a kitchen and a bath, additional bedrooms, a 12-by-24-foot living room, a storage or workroom, and any other rooms you want.

If you purchase two modules at once, the cost per square foot is much less than that of one module alone, since one entire wall has been eliminated. Naturally, the cost per module decreases in proportion to the number of modules initially purchased.

There are a number of variations in combinations available. A typical plan for a two-unit combination is shown here, with a brief explanation of the rooms and their uses.

Two-unit combination (above) is spacious and airy, with sliding glass doors and porch to the left, the main living room directly ahead, and kitchen equipment and bathroom are out of sight to the right.

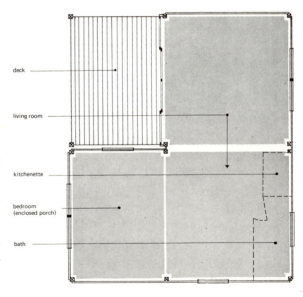

The current price for Unit One is just over $1,500; with front deck and porch, it is almost $2,000. The deck alone costs about $200 and the porch over $300.

Assembly by Work Crew. Not all precut packages are modeled to be assembled by the amateur builder, however. For example, Lindal Cedar Homes manufactures a number of inexpensive yet elegant precut second homes designed to be erected by work crews supplied by the manufacturer or by a contractor hired by the buyer.

The precut package does not cut out *all* labor costs in this case—the members of the work crew must be paid for their man-hours. However, the package does cut down on expenses, because the nature of the precut packages puts a ceiling on the amount of money spent on shaping material.

Preparation labor at the factory is included in the price of the precut materials. The man-hours involved in erecting the house on the building site is cut to a small percentage of conventional on-site labor cost; thus total labor expense is cut considerably.

You can purchase precut packages that include only the shell of the house, with the rest of the work left to you; or you can get precut packages that include the shell, the roughing-in, and all the finishing off.

Be sure you know exactly what you are getting.

Lindal Cedar Homes has several large precut homes available for the do-it-yourselfer who wants to see a work crew put up the shell of his second home but wants to have the finishing left to himself.

Sea Breeze is an extremely modern design for a leisure home, made possible by the use of post-and-beam construction. It is built of precut West Coast red cedar.

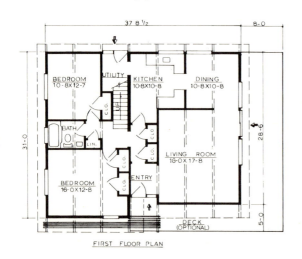

FIRST FLOOR PLAN

SECOND FLOOR PLAN

The McKinley is a large, livable, free-wheeling house for mountainous country.

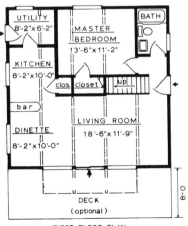

FIRST FLOOR PLAN

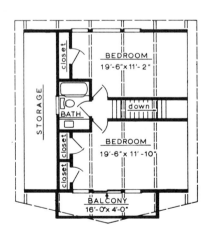

SECOND FLOOR PLAN

Sea Breeze delivers 1,784 square feet of living space, and costs around $13,000 standard. Other models run higher.

The Adriatic delivers 1,557 square feet of living space, and costs around $9,000 standard.

The McKinley delivers 1,468 square feet of living space, and costs over $9,000 standard.

The Adriatic is a modified A-frame made entirely out of West Coast red cedar precut before delivery to the building site.

Chapter 4

INTERLOCK CONSTRUCTION

ALTHOUGH interlock construction is actually a precut type of package, it is based on a principle different from the ordinary precut described in the preceding chapter.

In the conventional precut package, the pieces of lumber and framing timbers are fastened with ordinary nails, screws, and bolts.

In interlock construction, the pieces are actually shaped to interlock and are then fitted together so that the use of a nail, screw, or bolt reinforces the lock accomplished by the design.

THE LOG CABIN INTERLOCK

Of all the old-fashioned types of home construction, the log cabin is of course nearest and dearest to the heart of any American. The familiar shape of a log cabin in the woods is always a homey sight that brings back memories of the past, when the pioneer lived close to nature and hunted and fished in the good clean wilderness of the frontier. Somehow the log cabin satisfies something primeval in the human soul, something that parallels man's recent return to considerations of ecology and survival.

Horizontal logs interlocked at the corners give massive structural strength to any house or cabin, allowing it to withstand the elements and the depredations of woodland predators. It was because the early settlers understood this principle that most cabins in pioneer days were built of logs which were stacked and interlocked.

The log cabin is still the easiest kind of structure for the amateur to put together—provided, of course, the logs are shaped and carefully prepared to be fitted together in a perfect lock.

Precut Logs. Using the concept of the log cabin and combining it with precut materials, several precut firms have come up with log-cabin-type structures. These have the appearance and advantages of a modern house rather than an old-fashioned one. That is, they can support all modern utilities and will also keep out heat and cold more successfully than Abraham Lincoln's cabin did.

This type of vacation home can be erected quickly and easily by the amateur. All you do is assemble the precision-cut wooden parts packaged by the manufacturer.

There are many different designs of logs made for interlocking log-cabin structures, varying from those that look exactly like Lincoln logs to those that look exactly like ordinary shiplap siding. Most of these logs are made of cedar or pine.

The type of log cabin that looks most like a regular old-fashioned log cabin in the woods is made out of lodgepole pine, out of "Modelogs," full-round, solid logs prepared by Lumber Enterprises, Inc. and delivered ready for erection. The cabin is designed as an interlocking structure with stockade-type corners.

Lodgepole pine grows on the slopes of the Rocky Mountains. From these forests, mature trees that are straight and long and tough and strong are selected for cutting. Lodgepole pines are nature's most useful trees; they seem to be especially designed to make beautiful, stalwart, durable logs, as their name implies. The lodgepole was the center vertical of the Plains Indian's teepee.

Processing Lodgepole Logs. The first step in the processing of lodgepole timber into Modelog units is to remove the bark and peel the log mechanically. While this is being done, uniform roundness is established at the greatest possible diameter, ensuring minimum waste and therefore low cost. These construction logs are processed in diameters from six to nine inches—each size used in a different type of construction.

As the log is peeled, a deep groove is cut longitudinally into one side. This groove induces drying from both inside and outside simultaneously. Solid timber is commonly afflicted with splitting or checking when cured by external exposure only; the anticheck groove minimizes such splitting.

Modelogs come to site cut to size and ready to fit together. Fiberglass insulation is placed between the logs. Anticheck groove in log minimizes splitting. Tongue-and-groove joint runs lengthwise along each log. Many variations (opposite left) of this basic floor plan are available. Interior photograph (opposite right) shows lodgepole pine rafters and inside walls of natural logs.

Once the logs have dried, they are processed through precision machinery that planes them to a certain diameter; at the same time, they are given an accurate tongue-and-groove cutting. The bottom of each log is exactingly milled so that an extremely tight, weatherproof fit is assured as the logs are "layed" up. When the weight of the finished wall and the roof structure force the logs to compress (at points 1 and 2 in the drawing), a perfect seal is achieved.

Structural Properties. To ensure a total seal without any passage of air along the full length of each log, fiberglass insulation is placed between the logs, literally locking the units into a solid structure. No caulking whatsoever is needed.

This type of log-cabin structure is the closest thing to the kind used by pioneer families. The present design originated with craftsmen whose families through several generations scribed and hand-hewed logs for settlers' homes and other structures. The demand for hand-finished, tightly-fitted logs reached such a point that individual output could not supply enough. The company

then developed a machine to produce their logs on a volume basis, while retaining the natural character of hand-hewn work.

The pioneer logman's lost art is available today in many types of precut log cabins. The construction is popular for summer homes and woodland structures, as they are compatible with any natural surroundings.

The insulating efficiency of a solid-log wall is formidable, both for winter warmth and summer coolness. One inch of lodgepole pine has the insulating capacity of twelve inches of concrete. And solid log walls moderate humidity extremes as well as temperature variations, so that there is more uniform comfort and livability in a log cabin than in a conventional house.

Nothing ages as gracefully as a log-cabin structure, and the strength and stability inherent in the structure of the walls makes for a permanently solid, sound, and steadfast home.

The log itself is the entire thickness of the wall. You need to add no further interior wall surface, unless you prefer to. The log itself combines beautifully with other materials—stone, brick, mason, or other woods.

The natural-log interior wall goes well with darkstained beams against a white or brightly toned ceiling. Natural wood grain with intermittent knot formations is always pleasing to the eye and it cannot become dated.

Finishing off interior and exterior logs is easy. You just wipe on a clear finish and wipe off the soil or smudges.

The shell of the Modelog cabin shown runs about $3,500. Shells of vacation homes from Lumber Enterprises, Inc. run from just under $3,000 to $5,000 or more for a two-story model.

The St. Croix log-cabin vacation home of white cedar fits in admirably with the birch woods in this hillside setting.

Interior of white cedar cabin shows how knotty-pine partitions combine nicely with white cedar rafters and purlins above. Kitchen setup (right) blends brick, white pine, and inside surface of exterior white cedar wall.

WARD LOG CABINS

Many interlock vacation homes do not actually look like log cabins, although they are similar and are built up in exactly the same way. Ward Cabin Company, which uses white cedar in its logs, manufactures a log-cabin kit that you can put together almost like a child's toy.

Northern white cedar proved to be the most popular type of wood used by the frontiersmen in constructing their log cabins in the early Colonial days of America. White cedar provides an interesting rustic type of exterior for a home built in wooded terrain.

Each log is a section of peeled northern white cedar. The log is precut to the correct size, and is numbered and placed in a special bundle, with easy-to-understand instructions accompanying the material.

How to Build. No extra tools are needed to put up this interlock log cabin. You simply fit the tongue-and-groove logs together and build up the walls the way you would a brick wall, fitting in windows and doors as they come.

Each joint is especially mortised at the factory for a tight fit. The wall itself, from peeled outer exterior to planed interior, is about four inches thick. The accompanying diagrams show you how overlapping joints are fitted, and how interlocking corner joints are butted.

The vacation-home package you get includes all the outer shell of the cabin—walls, windows, doors, and roof, along with sills, girders, floor joist, subflooring, flooring, rafters, and roofboards. Transportation costs are not included in the price. Also not included are the foundation, the chimney, plumbing, wiring, paint, varnish, cabinets, and heating.

Laying up a Wall. To build a wall, you lay a 2¼-inch-by-7¾-inch sill and bolt it to the foundation wall. The bottom log run—a special type of log—is attached to the sill. Then each run of logs is attached to the one below, up to the roof line.

Each log has a tongue running along the top and a groove running along the bottom. To lay a run of logs, you simply smear the tongue of the already-laid row with caulking material and fit the second log's groove carefully onto the tongue.

Then you pound an 8-inch spike through both for a secure fit. Caulking makes the joints completely weatherproof. The inside surface of the log gives you a plain, smooth interior wall, resembling conventional informal knotty-pine surfacing. There is no space between interior and exterior wall surfaces; the wall is solid from outside to inside.

The cedar logs used do not run continuously from corner to corner. Short sections are butted together in a mortised locking end that prevents any weather leakage. All corner joints are fitted together with a type of interlocking mortise too.

Putting on the Roof. When you have finished the wall up to the roof line, you can either have a professional come in to put on the roof, or do it yourself. The vertical logs observed on the cabin ends running from the top horizontal log run to the pitched roof must be cut on site to fit. All the other logs are precut and prepared for a tight joint. Because of the interlocking feature of the construction, you must put up each house without any modifications in the basic floor plan.

Not all the cabins manufactured by this company feature horizontal logs. Some are designed with logs at the vertical. Vertical log cabins are constructed in exactly the same way as the horizontal ones.

Designs for Log Homes. While a small square or rectangular log cabin is the type you most often see in a wooded area, you can build a different, larger type of second home from the same precut log-type material. Designs of chalets, regular homes, and spacious vacation cottages are available not only from this company, but from many others as well.

All these log-cabin houses are based on the same type of wall construction. The more complicated designs are intended for erection by a professional builder.

By the very nature of the construction, the interiors of these log cabins are picturesque,

Small close-up shows two "logs" of laminated cedar being fitted together after precision cutting at factory. Three-ply decking material is made by Potlatch Forests. All components of the walls, floor, and roof are offered in package to build the leisure home shown at right. Interior is spacious and easy to keep up, leaving plenty of time for recreation, as in far right photograph.

rustic, and warm. Interior partitions are constructed of knotty pine, to match the exterior white cedar; the interiors have massive rafters hewn out of white cedar, and roughhewn purlins directly supporting the roof boards.

HOMES OF CEDAR

International Homes of Cedar's "log" is really not a log at all—that is, each piece of timber is not simply a cut, stripped, and notched unit of wood—but is rather a laminated, three-ply decking material of Western cedar manufactured by Potlatch Forests, Inc. Each log is actually a combination of three pieces of timber attached with adhesive, with the center board offset to form a tongue on one side and end, and a groove opposite for a tight fit.

This laminated decking material is similar to plywood, although of course the grain of the middle member does not run at right angles to the grain of the face members.

The laminated Potlatch log is held together by an exterior grade of adhesive which, under tremendous heat and pressure, welds these boards together into a permanent solid unit. Each "log" is three inches thick and consists of two 1-by-8-inch faces and a 1¼-by-8-inch core. Each piece is of course factory-machined and delivered to you ready for assembly.

Notched-Log Technique. The old frontier method of notching the logs for fitting at the corners has been followed in IHC's "Lock-Deck" timbers. The joint occurs at each corner and wall intersection.

Each joint is precision-machined on equipment made especially for that purpose. The joint locks the timbers together so tightly that you can assemble a house securely enough to live in without using any nails. Nails are provided, however, for additional support and to guarantee strength and rigidity.

Laminated Log Package. When you order a house of this type, you get a complete set of plans with the packaged material, along with a step-by-step guide that tells you exactly how to erect the house.

Everything is included in the package except the material and instructions for the foundation. Once you receive the plans, you build the foundation yourself or have someone construct it for you in accordance with the log cabin's specifications.

The interlock-type package includes all components for walls, floor, and roof. Each wall is lettered alphabetically, and each board has an individual mark to show exactly where it fits.

All you have to do is lay each laminated timber in the correct position and fit the marked parts together. The photographs show a house in various stages of construction.

Varied Designs of Homes. Several variations in design for houses of different sizes and shapes are available. In addition to the plans the company has on hand, you can ask them to design a custom plan for your own particular needs for a small extra sum.

Precut packages do not include foundation, plumbing, and wiring. However, the insulation qualities of three-inch laminated cedar are so high that you do not have to add any interior wall covering to the average structure. Since you can usually count on an airtight house, you do not have to plan to use extra money to cover emergency heating situations.

Where to Build Laminated Houses. Interlock structures can be used for the beach, for the mountains, for a valley or a flat plain; interlock can also be used for any vacation house of almost any size and design.

The advantage of an interlock house is speed, accuracy, and ease of assembly. You can usually do the job yourself, reducing labor costs and construction time to a minimum.

You can close in the house much faster than when you use uncut materials; all the on-site cutting and fitting are eliminated, thus reducing labor costs practically to zero.

Minimum Maintenance. As for maintenance on this type of structure, it is extremely low. The inherent strength and rigidity of the interlocking timbers gives the house greater strength than conventional construction or prefabrication.

Three-ply interlocking construction precludes the appearance of cracks, knots, and flaws. No settling cracks can appear, either, because of the tongue-and-groove design. All wood has been kiln-dried and will not shrink, warp, or check.

K-LODGE CABIN

Still another type of interlock cabin is available from K Products Corporation. Their K-Lodge Cabin comes in a do-it-yourself kit exactly like those described earlier in this chapter. Made of three plies of wood laminated together, the K-Lodge log interlocks like the logs in a conventional log cabin, with the run on one wall staggered with those on the wall at right angles to it.

The logs are made of precut western red cedar.

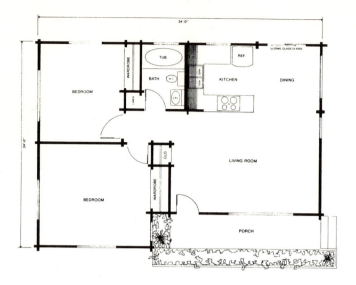

Photograph (opposite right) shows a K-Lodge in the process of construction. Artist's rendition (below) of a finished K-Lodge shows the Wells Fargo, with a living area of 736 square feet, or 816 square feet with porch. Cabin has real Western mountain feeling.

The tongue-and-groove concept makes them easy to assemble. Included in the construction kit—along with instructions—are partition material for inside the house, windows, prehung doors, floors, and roofing materials.

Small items like nails, trim molding, drain troughs, downspouts, and roof flashing are also included—everything needed for the shell.

WESTERN CEDAR LOGS

Exterior and interior wall partitions, ceilings, and doors require no finish or maintenance, but stand as you put them up. Each log is coded for easy matching.

The color of western cedar ranges from almost pure white to reddish-brown. Cedar is lightweight and has a long life. Its heartwood is highly resistant to decay and termites, because the timber produces a toxin that kills bacteria and small insects. It also possesses very good insulation qualities and can cut your heating bill considerably.

HOW TO BUILD A K-LODGE

To build this log cabin, you start with a conventional foundation such as a concrete wall, concrete block, or piles and girder. The rest is very easy, merely a matter of stacking the logs one on top of the other, staggering each run.

Concealed plumbing and electrical connections are installed. Pipes and wires run up from below the floor through vertical holes bored in the laminated logs as they are erected.

The roof, of Douglas fir, is designed to support snow-loading requirements in areas where snowfalls are exceptionally heavy. All outside and inside walls, except the plumbing wall, are constructed of heavy-duty laminated logs. Western cedar logs are kiln-dried, assembled with a tongue-and-groove construction, and have a special joint that locks out weather.

If the lot you own has a limited size or an irregular shape, the engineering department of K Products will work out a modified design.

Or, if you prefer to custom-design your own home, send in the floor plans and sketches, and the company's engineers will make working plans for a slight additional cost.

K Lodges come in many sizes with prices ranging from about $2,000 for a 240-square foot cabin, called the Bachelor Pad, through $10,000 or more for the 1,216-square-foot Super Chaparral.

Chapter 5

PREFABRICATED CONSTRUCTION

THE word "prefabricated" in relation to the building of homes has taken on such a wide variety of meanings that it is necessary to explain and redefine the use to which the word is put in this book.

The original definition of "prefabricate" in the dictionary is "to build a house in standardized sections for shipment and quick assembly." That definition, of course, is an extremely broad one that covers a multitude of situations.

SECTIONAL BUILDING

As can readily be seen, a prefabricated house is different from a precut house and an interlock house in that it is delivered to the building site in large prebuilt sections, called panels or components, rather than simply in bundles of lumber.

However, certain prefabricated houses are more prefabricated than others, and some are only very slightly prefabricated before shipment. A mobile home and a modular home—both of which are actually already completely built before they leave the factory—are prefabricated too, but they fall into another category, that of a "prefinished" home.

THE THREE GRADES OF PREFAB

A prefabricated home package always includes the material for the shell of the house. You can purchase a prefab that includes only the shell and nothing more. This type of prefab is called the "shell" prefab. You can also specify that you want a particular prefabricated house erected only through the shell stage if you choose.

The erected shell prefab is a weathertight structure built on a specified foundation, with studded partitions, insulation, stairs, and decks all in place. Interior doors and trim for final installation at the finished house stage are usually supplied with the erected shell, although none of this is assembled.

A prefabricated home package can include all plumbing, heating, and wiring in addition to the shell. In the building trade a house consisting of shell, plumbing, heating, and wiring is said to be in the "rough-finish" stage. A prefab delivered with plumbing, heating, and electricity is called the rough-finish prefab.

The rough-finish prefab is a house in a livable

stage, including erected shell, with plumbing, electricity, and heating installed, but without wall finish.

One type of prefab which is currently gaining popularity is the rough-finish prefab that has the plumbing, heating, and wiring in a special portion within the prefab package, a portion called the "mechanical core." A prefab delivered with the core is called the mechanical-core prefab. It is of course only one special type of rough-finish prefab.

A prefabricated home that is delivered with everything finished—shell, rough finishing, and final finishing—is called a "finished" prefab.

The finished prefab is a house complete and ready for immediate occupancy, with all trim installed, all surfaces painted, and with carpeting in place and all fireplace and other masonry work done.

Know What You Are Getting. There are many degrees of completion other than these three stages—shell, rough-finish, and finished prefab—but for the sake of discussion these three should give you an accurate idea of what to look for in the typical prefab package.

Many firms will sell you a prefab delivered at any one of the three stages mentioned, with correspondingly different prices. Thus, you can choose a shell prefab of a certain design and model, or if you want a rough-finish home, you can order exactly that.

The main point is to be sure of exactly what you are getting. You should have an itemized list and be familiar with this list before you pay any money.

Opposite page, top to bottom: Workmen in the process of lowering a prefabricated side wall onto an already laid foundation and constructed floor for attachment to the front and back walls of house. A bird's-eye view of workmen installing a mechanical core, including bathroom and kitchen pipes and wires along with fixtures and appliances. Bottom photograph shows the roof already half assembled on the rest of the shell. Note the insulation in the roof panels; all this work has been done at the factory before shipment to the site. The photograph above shows the fully assembled, finished house. Final phases of finishing off have been done in erected shell.

No Foundation. The average prefab does not include a foundation. The wide variety of natural terrain and the broad range of geological problems encountered in the fifty states preclude the furnishing of a standard foundation for all areas. You are required to supply the foundation yourself or have it put in by a subcontractor. In many cases the builder supplying the prefab will send ahead a crew of men to put in the foundation for you, but you will be charged for the materials and the labor.

Let's take up these three broad types of prefabs one by one to see how each is erected.

The "Shell" Prefab. The first step in any prefab is the laying of the foundation. Then the floor is attached to the foundation. Sometimes the floor is composed of precut lumber; sometimes it may consist of prefabricated panels that are attached to the foundation.

Once the floor has been laid, the second step in the building of the house is the raising of the walls. The walls have been built—sometimes with all interior surfaces finished, sometimes not—at the factory. These sections are then held upright and nailed into place on the flooring.

The third step is the enclosing of the shell by the roof. The roof sections are put in place, and the entire house is then covered with roof sheathing. Simultaneously windows, doors, and locks are installed in the walls of the shell—provided they are not already prebuilt into the components.

At this point the shell is finished. In some cases, the interior walls are already in place; in others, the interior walls must follow after the roughing-in of the plumbing and electric wiring.

The "Rough-Finish" Prefab. Some prefabricated houses include the shell *and* the plumbing, electricity, and heating roughed into the walls. When a home is delivered in this fashion, it is called a rough-finish house.

Obviously the rough-finish prefab is not the house to put up in the wilds away from utilities and conveniences, but rather to erect in a more settled area or in a vacation community.

The rough-finish prefab does not include painting, plastering, carpeting, and so on.

The "Mechanical-Core" Prefab. Certain rough-finish prefab packages include the plumbing, electricity, and heating already in the prefabricated walls that come from the factory, along with plumbing fixtures, heating units, and electrical appliances that operate on these pipes and wires.

This portion of a prefab package is called the mechanical core. It is delivered in two parts: (1) the wiring and plumbing in the walls; (2) the appliances, heaters, and plumbing fixtures ready to be hooked to the wall components.

The mechanical core has one advantage: it establishes a ceiling price for all subcontracting and for all fixtures and components. A workman sent by the prefab company will hook up the mechanical core internally, and will then hook up the house to the proper utility systems on the building site.

The "Finished" Prefab. After the shell has been erected and the plumbing and electricity have been roughed in, the "finishing up" of the house follows.

Finishing up includes hooking up all appliances to the proper outlets, finishing off the walls with plaster, wallpaper, or paint, applying molding and trim to all areas in need of it, laying carpeting or tile where indicated, and finishing brickwork and masonry on fireplace, mantelpiece, or outside walls.

The finished prefab comes to you exactly in the same condition that a normal house erected by conventional methods comes to you: with all interior furnishing completed and the house in livable condition.

As you can see, the types of prefab houses vary from the simple shell prefab, which includes only the outer walls, floor, and roof, through the rough-finish prefab, with subcontractors supplying plumbing, heating and electricity, to the finished prefab, which includes everything a conventional house has.

THE SHELL PREFAB: "DO-IT-YOURSELF"

Actually, for the do-it-yourselfer, the shell prefab is the preferred package. That is, if you are a small-percentage do-it-yourselfer and don't want to handle any carpentry work of a critical nature—studs, rafters, joists, and so on—the shell prefab is exactly what the doctor ordered.

Once the shell is in place, you can step in and finish off the interior at your leisure: attaching interior wall surfaces, finishing the floor, ceilings, and tiling, and then doing the painting or papering of the entire house as you come to it.

A prefab is such a versatile type of house that you can almost always find one that suits your particular taste and skills. Of course, a prefabricated house, by its very nature, is a predesigned house that may contain a few variations but is generally locked into a basic stock design.

It goes without saying that the average prefabricated house is going to be more elaborate and considerably more expensive than the rugged shack-in-the-woods type you can put up strictly for roughing it in the boondocks. Most leisure houses of this type, in fact, can be used on a year-round basis.

There are literally dozens of manufacturers of prefabricated houses—some marketing their houses on a nation-wide basis, and other marketing them only in certain regional areas. Prices range from very inexpensive to very expensive. Quality varies from cheap to superior.

Let's take a look at some of the more popular examples of prefabs. From them you can get a fairly good idea of what kind you can look for in your own area.

Pease Homes. The Pease Company manufactures a shell prefab vacation house that you can either put up yourself or have put up by a work crew supplied by Pease.

The vacation homes pictured on these pages are precut houses, actually, but they also are prefabricated to a degree. That is, the Pease prefab is not totally assembled on the building site, but is shipped in panel sections called components, already put together at the factory, with fittings available for attachment to another component.

The design of the house breaks up into sectional components. Several panels make up the exterior of the house. The interior walls are also preassembled and are open for easy installation of wiring, heating, and plumbing. The roughing-in is left to you or to a subcontractor you can hire.

The Pease house can be put up in a weekend, either by a group of amateurs or by professionals.

Careful study of these leisure home drawings will show that each is designed for simple sectional assembly.

Then you can spend the rest of the season completing the inside to your satisfaction.

The shell does not include interior wall surfacing or interior paritions. You can put these up yourself at your leisure. The Pease package also does not include foundation or masonry materials, interior paneling and ceiling, plumbing and plumbing fixtures, wiring and electrical fixtures, insulation, heating and flues, linoleum, painting or decorating, gutters, and field labor.

A small one-bedroom module will cost just over $4,000 if you put it up yourself and are satisfied with only the shell.

Aladdin Homes. The granddaddy of prefabricated home manufacturers is the Aladdin Company, which has been in the business of supplying regular houses and second homes with prebuilt and precut parts since 1906.

The Delta is one of its many designs of inexpensive year-round or vacation houses. The price for the Aladdin package on this house is a little over $6,000 for Delta #1, and close to $6,500 for Delta #2—the difference being in the floor plan and the shape and size of the house.

Aladdin's package includes all framing material from girder sill through rafters—floor joists, subfloor, preassembled exterior walls with sheathing applied, preassembled partitions, wood siding, exterior trim, and so on, as well as roof shingles, preassembled windows, prehung inside doors, inside trim, three coats of paint/varnish/stain, erection drawings, book of instructions, nails, and locksets.

The package does not include erection labor, heating, plumbing, wiring, or masonry materials. That means you will have to build your own foundation and supply your own wiring and electrical fixtures and heating and plumbing items. Brickwork on any Aladdin home is not included either.

Since you can either build it yourself or have it built for you, you can save money by using Aladdin's package. Mill labor is cheaper than field labor; you know definitely what your materials will cost in advance.

Actually, an Aladdin is a precut *and* premanufactured package. The exterior walls are preassembled with sheathing applied and contain precut openings for windows and doors. To erect, you simply place and nail. The dimensions are so accurate that you should have no difficulty; just follow the drawings carefully.

Windows are preassembled with sash applied. They fit the openings provided for in the exterior

The Delta can be situated either on a small plot of land or on a section of ground that is awkwardly shaped. Compactness and versatility are keynotes to this year-round second home—for leisure, vacation, or retirement.

wall panels. Inside window trim is precut, packaged, and made for proper application. Average installation time runs fifteen to twenty minutes apiece. Storm sash are also available, factory-applied, if ordered with house materials.

Inside doors are prehung with latches applied. A quality flush birch door is used and precut, packed trim is included.

Floor joists, ceiling joists, bridging, rafters, and so on are precut and marked for proper application. All that is necessary is to note the marking on the item to be applied, look in the construction drawings for the proper location, and then place and nail. Construction is made easy through Aladdin's step-by-step procedure, perfected through the years.

Stair stringers, treads, and risers are also precut. You need spend no time figuring complicated runs and rises; after cutting the stringers to length, just place them and nail.

Aladdin has a custom manufacturing department, so if you cannot find a plan that you like in their catalog, you can send in a special plan and the engineering department will price it for you with no extra charge. The price will carry the standard precut specifications and will carry the usual guarantee.

You can build an Aladdin home on a regular foundation or on a concrete slab. You can also procure standard foundation plans as soon as you pay a deposit on a house.

THE "ROUGH FINISH" PREFAB

A rough-finish prefab is manufactured by Wausau Homes. It is a mechanical-core prefab

The Rochester is a versatile home that can is suitable as a retirement home or as a starter home for young marrieds, or it can serve as a leisure home in a vacation community.

model shipped to the building site in sections and then assembled by a team of four men in about 100 to 150 working hours.

You can get a fairly clear picture of how the average prefab is put together by studying the pictures included here. These panels, or sections, are all built indoors under controlled temperature and humidity conditions, with both exterior and interior wall panels delivered to the site closed, insulated, and wired. The kitchen/bathroon unit comes as a mechanical core, complete with all plumbing, heating, and electrical units installed.

The Weston. An affiliate company of Wausau Homes, called Weston Homes, also produces mechanical-core prefabs. One of their leisure homes and its floor plan is shown here.

The mechanical-core prefab does not allow the do-it-yourselfer much latitude, but it does afford him a home that can be assembled—complete—in a matter of days by professional carpenters and mechanics.

THE "FINISHED" PREFAB

If you are in the market for a more elaborate house than you would need for a summer or winter place, you should probably plan to buy a four-season "finished" house.

Great Northern Homes has twelve basic plans to choose from, one of which is called simply The Life House. This two-story structure is weatherproof and season-proof as well, and is handsomely designed for year-round living as well as for seasonal enjoyment.

The finished package the company offers is a completed, ready-for-occupancy house. The unit is supplied in its entirety by the builders, without any work for you to do.

The full package includes foundation, shell, interior finish, winterizing, plumbing, electricity, stain, and so on. It is not a do-it-yourself house at all, but a spacious, livable home delivered into your hands finished and ready for immediate occupancy.

As you can see by a glance at the plan, this

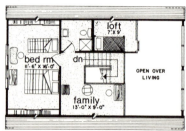

The Life House is a perfect year-round house for almost any kind of weather. It is a two-story structure with 3 bedrooms and 1½ baths.

is a house that has plenty of living space, with expansion room available if you need it. The main features of the house are:

Maintenance-free redwood exterior
Bronze-framed windows and doors
A spacious kitchen and dining area
A sizable family room and loft

The steep peaked roof gives the house the look of a large A-frame, although it is stretching the truth to categorize it as an A-frame. Yet it has the advantages of the A and its woodsy, casual look.

There are many obvious benefits to the plan for this home:

1. The 4/12 roof angle minimizes ice buildup on the roof edges that might cause inside leaks, a particularly valuable feature in an area where there is a great deal of snow and ice.

2. The double-thickness flooring—2-inch tongue-and-groove white plank—cuts down the possibility of shrinkage and gives you a stronger floor system.

3. The redwood exterior gives you resistance to termites, greater durability, and less maintenance.

4. The full-size complete kitchen gives you pleasant surroundings for preparation of meals and greater versatility in dining.

5. Bronzed windows and doors that are weather-stripped and lockable will give you higher insulation value and greater security.

The house utilizes windproof shingles, large overhangs to prevent injury to exterior walls, post-and-beam construction throughout, huge glass areas for better viewing and sunlight, and beamed ceilings.

Winterizing materials include 1-inch urethane roof insulation, 3-inch fiberglass wall insulation, and 1-inch floor insulation, with a standard gas, oil, or electric heating system.

This home can be brought in for approximately $20 per square foot of living area, excluding the decks that surround the house. Most of the homes designed and built by the company start in the neighborhood of $20,000 fully finished.

The company arranges a meeting with you as soon as you express interest in a home, so that you can meet a local builder-dealer for a careful on-site inspection of your chosen lot. You can name your contractor if you wish.

The builder will also sponsor you at one of the lending institutions that service your area with mortgages. This home meets the National Building Code and is acceptable for conventional as well as FHA financing.

Great Northern Homes has builder-dealers nationwide, but their primary market area is in the northeast region of the United States, from Ohio eastward and Georgia northward.

Acorn Structures. Another manufacturer supplying finished prefab vacation homes is Acorn Structures. In its price list, Acorn gives three different stages of construction to choose from: "erected shell," "rough-finish," or "finished house."

To quote three prices on one of their model houses, the finished house price is $15,000; the rough-finish house is $12,000; and the erected shell is $8,800. A comparison of these figures should give you some idea of the spread between the cost of a shell prefab and a finished prefab from any company.

The Saltbox. One of the most interesting of all Colonial home designs is the saltbox, a structure that appeared in the middle of the seventeenth century around New England. The shape of the saltbox house is unmistakable even today.

It has a long and honorable history. A pre-Revolutionary design, it came with built-in ad-

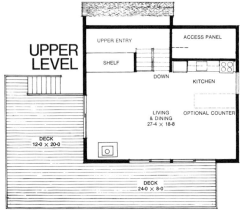

The Salt Box II is designed with classic New England lines and a typically nonsymmetrical roof. This is a two-level house, with the upper living area open to the lower living area.

vantages: it saved on roofing material, and it saved on heat. It was thus perfectly suited to the penny-pitching Yankees who populated North America at that time.

The saltbox is a two-story house in front and a one-story house in the rear. Because of this odd architectural quirk, the profile of the saltbox is unique. Viewed from the gable ends, the short front roof and the long, slanting back roof give it the appearance of the type of salt container then prevalent in New England. Actually, a candle box of the time had the same shape, but "candle-box house" apparently didn't sound right.

The design helped save on roof expense; the back roof actually acted as a back wall, too. And by building the house facing south, the back roof wall took the brunt of winter storms from the north and northeast, saving heat and shedding snow easily.

The historical saltbox has a large room to one side of the front door on the main level, and above this room a large bedchamber. Another room extends from behind the first floor to the slope, or "lean-to," section of the roof. Some old saltboxes have a loft above part of the back room, which served as sleeping space for the children.

Acorn Structures prefab saltbox reverses the old design by flipping the floor plan—that is, what was downstairs in the old saltbox is upstairs; and what was upstairs in the old saltbox is downstairs.

The Salt Box II, shown in the photograph, is a 24-by-28 foot structure, with a total of 1,232 square feet of living space. It has 3 bedrooms and 1½ baths.

UPPER LEVEL

LOWER LEVEL

The Nutshell 900 is a complete, family-sized house with two large bedrooms and a bunk room. It will, if challenged, sleep ten people. The balcony upstairs looks out onto a cathedral-ceilinged living room—which has 16 feet of glass—opening out onto an airy deck and any view you have: mountain, lake, sea, plains, desert.

The erected shell comes to around $15,000, with the finished house running about $25,000. Acorn Structures services the East Coast, broadly speaking, with some activity in the Middle West and the South.

Nutshell 900. This Acorn house is a complete family-size home with two large bedrooms and a bunk room. It has a saltbox appearance from the side, but is not actually a saltbox at all.

Small enough and compact enough for two people, it will sleep ten in a pinch. It is thus excellent for vacation use.

A balcony above looks out on a cathedral-ceiling living room. The living room has a 16-foot glass window opening out onto a large deck where you can enjoy a view of the sea, a lake, or a mountain from inside or out.

The Nutshell 900 is a 24-by-28-foot structure, with a total of 912 square feet of living space. It has 3 bedrooms and 1 bath. The erected shell comes to just over $11,000; the finished house comes to $20,000 or more.

Chapter 6

MOBILE HOMES

In addition to second homes that you can build all or partially by yourself, there are those that you can buy ready to move into. Some you can even buy with the interior furnishings supplied in their entirety.

The smallest—and least expensive—of these finished second homes can be delivered "as is" to your lot in its entirety, finished off from floor to ceiling. It is a fairly new adaptation of another type of American specialty, the mobile home.

Actually, the latest model of the mobile home is not "mobile" at all, but "immobile" most of the time; it should really be called a "relocatable" home. This particular type of home fills a growing need for less expensive models of second homes. In many cases this home acts not as a second home at all, but as a temporary first or permanent retirement home.

Early mobile-home designs twenty years ago were developed as trailer homes, furnished like camping trailers and intended for use in a "roughing-it" style of life.

The mobile home that has evolved from the old trailer unit now has all the modern conveniences of any year-round house and is designed to function as a genuine minimum housekeeping unit.

There are more than two million mobile homes in the country now, housing five million people. One in every four families that buys a house buys a mobile home.

As a vacation home, the mobile home stands midway between the conventional cabin or house—the second home—and the modern camper on wheels. It is smaller and less versatile than the ordinary first home, but is more elaborate and larger than either the camper or the trailer house designed to be towed by an automobile.

Because of its size and weight, commonly 12 feet wide by 65 feet long, it is towed to the site by truck, set on a prepared base, and then stripped of its wheels and axles.

Most units are boxcar-shaped, similar to suburban ranch houses. Usually designed to include living room, dining and kitchen area, 2 bedrooms, bath and closets, the average mobile home can serve very well as a conventional vacation home.

Some models consist of two units joined together to make a larger leisure home. Many have expandable sections, with extra rooms available that can be added to most units.

The obvious advantage of the mobile home

as a second, leisure, or vacation home is its cost ceiling. The entire house is included in the price—not only the outer shell, but the interior decorations and all built-in furnishings as well.

Maintenance is kept at a minimum. Most exteriors are aluminum with a baked-enamel finish that can be hosed down and almost never needs repairing or repainting. Inside surfaces of Formica and vinyl make for easy cleaning. Each mobile home unit has full insulation and central heating.

There is one thing to understand and keep in mind about mobile homes, however. Because these homes have not always been as good-looking and as versatile as they are today, many communities have passed statutes outlawing the mobile home within the borders of their towns and cities.

The versatile mobile home can be hauled and set down almost anywhere. Small shrubs keep the skirting in the background and disguise the fact that the house is a mobile home.

Interior of the typical mobile home shows how maintenance is kept at a minimum. Surfaces of Formica and vinyl make the furnishings easy to clean.

Special areas, mobile-home parks or camps, have been set aside in these communities for mobile homes. Many of these parks are filled to capacity during most seasons of the year.

When a developer opens up a new park, you can then reserve a space in it for your mobile home. However, the developer may be a mobile-home dealer himself, in business to sell them. If you have already purchased a mobile home, he may not let you settle in his park.

Therefore, do not purchase a mobile home unless you have already arranged for a place to put it. It is difficult to get rid of a mobile home that does not have a parking place—difficult if not impossible.

SIZES OF MOBILE HOMES

The mobile home today has such a wide variety of designs, sizes, and prices that almost any family, regardless of size or income, can find one to suit its needs.

The mobile home is generally 12 feet wide by 65 feet long, with heavier units sometimes 14 feet wide. Prices range from $5,000 to $12,000, but the average is $7,000. Many of these homes can be financed by savings and loan companies, and FHA, VA, or Farmers Home Administration will insure loans.

A mobile home provides living quarters for a family of two or three. The actual overall living area in a 12-by-65-foot mobile home is 12 by 62 feet, or 744 square feet. The 3-by-12-foot area lost is taken up by a 3-foot towing hitch.

Interior designs vary, but the average 12-by-65-foot mobile home contains a living room, a kitchen-dining area, one or two bathrooms, and one or two bedrooms.

Furnishings included in the purchase price of the mobile home are as follows: draperies, carpeting or area rugs, range, refrigerator, water heater, furnace, hardwood cabinets, bathtub, shower, lavatory, living-room furniture, dinette furniture, and bedroom furniture. Optional items include air conditioning, garbage disposal, washer and dryer, dishwasher, and fireplace.

Certain designs of mobile homes have expandable sections that telescope into the shell while it is being towed and pull out into place when the home is on site. An expandable section can add 60 to 80 square feet (6 by 10 feet) of living space to either living room or bedroom, and gives the home a ranch house look.

14-wide: 14 by 64 feet—896 square feet.

12-wide: 12 by 64 feet—768 square feet.

12-wide expandable: 12 by 58 expandable—696 up to 815 square feet.

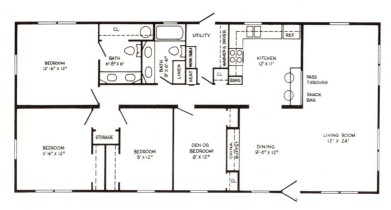

Double-wide: 24 by 49—1,176 square feet.

Add-a-room units can also be purchased separately and attached to the house after it is in place. From 150 to 300 square feet of living space can be added by this method.

A double-wide mobile home is composed of two or more sections shipped separately and joined together on the homesite. Double-wides cost between $9,000 and $19,000, and they provide 3 bedrooms, 1 or 2 bathrooms, living room, dining room, kitchen, and a utility room.

A mobile home costs approximately $8.75 per square foot for both home and furnishings.

The 14-by-60-foot mobile homes being manufactured now afford 840 square feet of living space; they are permitted to be moved in less than half the states.

There are mobile homes especially designed as vacation homes. These are styled for easy care and maintenance, and some are built with sharply sloping roofs to shed snow and rain in mountain or lake retreats.

FINANCING YOUR MOBILE HOME

Mobile homes are easy to finance, according to Robert L. Wallace of C.I.T. Financial Services. You simply purchase a mobile home as you would purchase an automobile—with a down payment plus regular monthly installments.

Most of the time the financing is arranged for you by the dealer from whom you purchase the home. He will help you obtain financing either

Left: These four mobile home floor plans are representative of those found within each of the major style and size categories, including 12-wide, 14-wide, 12-wide expandable, and double-wide homes.

from a finance company or a bank, or possibly from a savings and loan association.

The handling of financial arrangements for the purchase of a mobile home is much easier than those for the purchase of a conventional home. Additional costs, such as attorney fees and title searches, are avoided. Approval of the buyer's credit usually comes within a few hours after the decision to buy has been made—quite a contrast to conventional home buying.

TYPICAL COSTS OF A MOBILE HOME

Here is a typical example of mobile-home financing costs:

Basic home price	$5,600
Down payment	$1,120
Balance to be financed	$4,480
Monthly payments (5 years)	$97.07 per month
Total cost (60 payments)	$6,944

In the case above, a 20 percent down payment and an add-on finance charge of 6 per cent per year have been used. Both these figures can vary. When the total cost of the mobile home is higher, a lower-percentage down payment is required, and the monthly payments may be spread over a longer term than five years.

In the past, interest usually has been quoted on the basis of a "discount" or "add-on." It still is, but it now must include the translation of these terms into the simple interest rate.

You will find this simple interest stated in your contract, and you should understand what it is even though it may not be as important to you as the figure of what you will have to pay monthly.

The Consumer Credit Protection Act, which became effective July 1, 1969, did not lower the cost of borrowing money or of financing the purchase of any items, including mobile homes. It has no effect on the actual interest rate. The act protects consumers, however, because it is driving out of business unregulated credit organizations that may have been charging such exorbitant simple interest rates as 25 or 30 percent.

You can, of course, buy a mobile home entirely for cash, and save yourself all interest charges. But many people, even when they have the cash, prefer to buy on installment and thereby conserve their cash for any emergencies that may arise.

There is one other method of financing a mobile home, provided you own land zoned for real estate and plan to keep your mobile home permanently on this land. Some mortgage institutions will make the same type of loan on the mobile home as they would on a conventional home. You might, however, find it difficult to locate such a mortgage institution.

Some mobile homes meet the specifications of the Federal Housing Administration and government financing assistance for homes to be located in rural areas may be obtained through the Farmers Home Administration, Washington, D.C.

When you buy your mobile home, you should review with your dealer all the insurance coverage you might want on it. This fee can be paid on the installment plan if you so desire.

Artist's rendering (above) shows a brand-new design for a mobile home that is a departure from the conventional boxcar shape. An angular conservatory ends with full-length awning-type windows which open up inside space and establish relationship with the exterior. Interior view (below) shows the living room of the same mobile home.

You may wish to insure not only the house itself against various accidents, but also the personal belongings you have in it. The extent of the coverage will be up to you, and of course the cost will vary proportionally.

While most mobile homes are not transported from one site to another, and you may have no intention of ever moving it at the time you buy, it is a good idea to be certain that your financing source will permit you to make such a move.

Most financial institutions will let you move, provided you have made all payments according to your contract and you let them know where you are going with the mobile home.

Over the years the average cost of financing a mobile home has grown. Partly this rise reflects higher costs and larger homes, but it also reflects easier credit terms. It is a tribute to the average man's financial common sense that the number of delinquencies on mobile-home debt remains very small.

Mobile home life is a way of life for both the young and the old; financial institutions are making every possible effort to enable more people to experience its pleasures.

HOW TO SELECT A MOBILE-HOME PARK

The selection of a site for a mobile home differs somewhat from the selection of a site for a conventional vacation home. You cannot expect to bring a mobile home to an area that already has a number of conventional vacation homes erected; there are usually zoning laws which forbid it.

If you find a remote spot of your own, which

This typical mobile home park shows good management and illustrates the advantages of restrictions against sloppiness and carelessness: lawns kept trimmed, plants well tended, space between each home and roadway, driveways adequate, skirting hiding ugly underpinnings.

is not subject to zoning laws, you can bring in a mobile home and set it up in any fashion you desire. However, you must consider the problem of bringing in electric power and taking care of plumbing problems.

Because of these utility considerations, it is the usual procedure to settle a mobile home in a mobile-home park. There are more than 22,000 of these parks in the United States at the present time, some with as few as twelve or fifteen sites, and some with several hundred lots.

In a mobile-home park, you will be expected to pay a monthly rental of from $25 to $100 for the site, depending on the location and the services available.

Some mobile-home parks sell lots instead of renting them. You will then own your site, subject to certain restrictions, and you will pay a fee for services and park maintenance instead of the rental payment on the lot. Cooperative mobile-home parks also exist, which operate like co-op apartment houses.

In searching for a mobile-home park, there are several points you must consider:

1. *Size of the lot.* The most important thing to determine right away is the space allotted to each home. You do not want to feel cramped if you are used to a lot of space; contrarywise, you do not want too much space to take care of.

2. *Parking spaces.* Be sure to find out whether there are one or perhaps two parking spaces available on each lot. You do not want to turn away guests for lack of parking space.

3. *Space for patio or garden.* If you are used to having lounging space near your home, you must be sure such space is available. And if you want a garden, you must find out if there is room for one.

4. *Electric power supply.* If you have a totally electric home, you must find out if there is adequate current provided to operate it. You would also have to add more wattage if you have an air-conditioning unit. Most parks usually provide at least 100 amps of service for each home. A minimum of 150 amps, however, is required if your home is totally electric. Many new parks provide 200 amps of service for all spaces. Some even go up to 250 amps.

5. *Restrictions.* Watch out for restrictions—or the lack of them. Too many restrictions make life unbearable. Too few may make it unpleasant. Each mobile home in a park should be required to be skirted, and the props that hold up the home should be covered by some kind of metal cover. If these regulations are not enforced, the park is much too permissive.

Low-maintenance landscaping in front of this mobile home shows how the judicious use of small shrubs and plants saves the owner the trouble of mowing a large expanse of lawn.

6. *Recreational facilities.* Some parks have clubhouses available for all who live there. Others have a minimum of recreational facilities. Before you sign a contract, find out as much as you can about the park. Talk to people who live there and size them up to see if they will be compatible.

7. *Size of mobile home lot.* You can judge the site of the lot fairly easily. If you are planning on a double-wide home—20 by 24 feet wide—the lot size must be proportionately larger than it would be for a 12- or 14-foot-wide home.

LANDSCAPING

Because all mobile homes tend to be similar in shape and form—even the expandables and doubles resemble boxcars—you must pay a great deal of attention to the type of landscaping nec-

essary to make the home fit into its environment.

Pay attention also to the use of low-maintenance landscaping materials. The lawn of a suburban house can be difficult to maintain. In a mobile home park, however, the lawn is much smaller, and can be kept in near perfect condition with very little work.

In the borders next to the walls of the home and under shrubs and flower beds, use plenty of stone or bark mulch. The mulch will cut down on weeds and will save you a great deal of clipping and trimming.

If you do not fancy lawn work of any kind, use ground-cover plants and low or creeping shrubs to hide the bare dirt. If there are areas of the terrain that will not grow anything, build rock gardens or use shallow plastic pools of water to break up the monotony.

Since most mobile-park rules demand skirting, try to keep the skirting and screening of the undercarriage of the home as clean as possible. To cover the tinny utilitarian look, plant small shrubs and bushes beside the house to cover up the skirting.

On the border of the lot, plant shrubs or flower borders, using plants which will retain the shape and size you want. Do not overplant, or you will spend much of your time pruning back.

Plant annual flowers in the spring to obtain bright colors throughout the summer. Perennials and flowering plants will bloom for years. You can even put in a small vegetable garden in a sunny, sheltered place.

For shade, use a small tree, especially a medium-to-small-sized one to maintain the right proportion to the silhouette of the mobile home.

A tree too high will accentuate the boxcar shape of the structure. Plant the tree where it will give the shade or the screen you want, and will not cut off a good view. An unsightly view from your windows can be hidden by a fence or a high hedge.

Trellises are available for climbing vines and flowers. You can put up awnings to afford shade for a favorite sitting area.

EXTRAS

Unfortunately, many extras are necessary which are not included in the total cost of the mobile home. You really cannot get along without them. The cost of the items mentioned in this section should run between 10 to 15 percent of the cost of the mobile home.

1. *Concrete runners.* Foundation strips called concrete runners are 4 by 12 inches in girth and 60 feet long. They are placed 56 inches apart and parallel to form a double-railed level platform on which the mobile home can sit. The runners prevent the mobile home from settling into the ground. A runner should be cast with reinforced steel bars to increase the flexibility of the concrete strip.

2. *Cement blocks.* Cement building blocks are usually stacked on top of all concrete runners about eight to ten feet apart. The blocks are then topped with a shim—of adjustable thickness—on which the steel I beams of the mobile home's flooring rest. Most manufacturers furnish a chart that indicates where the blocks should be placed for best results.

3. *Piers and jacks.* In some instances, concrete

piers are used in place of concrete runners for mobile home foundations. Holes 12 to 18 inches in diameter are dug into the ground along the two I beams that make up the bottom of the mobile home; the holes are dug at intervals of eight to ten feet. These holes are then filled with concrete. Small jacks placed on these concrete piers support the I beams of the mobile home.

4. *Skirting.* Skirting is any kind of material used to cover and hide the wheels, blocks, and the open area under the mobile home. Skirting also provides weather protection for the home. You can install skirting in such a manner that it provides both proper ventilation and easy access to the area under the home.

5. *Steps.* A full set of steps is mandatory to provide access to each outside door of a mobile home. Since each home has at least two outside doors, and some three, the appearance and quality of these steps is important. A set of steps should be wide enough so that two or three people can stand on it at the same time. If possible, each set of steps should have a set of handrails.

Addition of rail-and-post fence here has given this mobile home site a great deal of added landscaping vitality. Dwarf tree in planter can be moved anywhere.

Outdoor living area around this mobile home is stretched out to blend in with the surrounding terrain with a combination of Western wood screens, decks, benches, and walkways enhanced with careful landscaping.

6. *Storage shed.* Since the storage space inside a mobile home is minimal, you should purchase an out-of-doors enclosure of metal to store gardening tools, bicycles, lawn furniture, and paints.

7. *Tie-down anchors.* To keep the mobile home erect during a storm, you should provide over-the-roof ties or frame ties, or a combination of both, in any area subject to high winds, heavy storms, or hurricanes. You can anchor these ties to the ground by a screw augur, an expanding prefabricated "dead man," or by means of precast concrete anchor blocks. Such anchors must be provided; a mobile home rests on its foundation; it is not secured to it, as is a conventional home.

8. *Refuse collection stand.* Every mobile home needs a concrete or masonry structure accommodating at least two regular garbage cans. The walls of the stand should be made of hollow-core

blocks so that the cans get proper ventilation. This stand will prevent dogs from knocking over garbage and trash cans, as well as hide them from the eye.

9. *Insurance.* You can usually insure your mobile home at the time you purchase it. If you already have an insurance agent, he can help you obtain the best protection. Insurance loss should be provided for the following contingencies: fire, flood, lightning, hail, explosion, riots, civil commotion, theft, vandalism, and window breakage.

You can also insure your own personal belongings by the purchase of a type of insurance called "personal effects protection."

PRODUCTION OF THE MOBILE HOME

The secret of the mobile home's inexpensiveness is its rapid-fire assembly-line production. In custom construction, the workers usually take their time—marking materials, cutting them, and then carefully fitting them into place for an overall custom effect. In a factory, there is a mechanized pacing that is astonishing to behold.

All lifting is done by power, rather than tediously by hand, as on a building site. Overhead hoists set walls in place in instants; on a building site it takes four men to push the frame for a wall into place.

Some assembly lines start with a steel-floor frame and end up with a complete, furnished home in twenty minutes.

Actually, the factory-built house is now entering its third phase. When mobile-home builders began supplying these houses for the public, most mobile homes were moved once or twice each year. Now they are rarely moved at all from their original site.

So—why not build other kinds of homes in "modules," or sections each resembling a mobile home, and then assemble these modules on site in a few hours?

No reason why not. The next chapter briefly discusses modular homes, and then presents several examples of modular housing both in the building stages and being lived in.

Chapter 7

MODULAR CONSTRUCTION

WHAT has come to be called the "modular" home package is simply a combination of a prefabricated-home package and a mobile-home package. Also called "sectionalized" construction, this type of home building differs from the prefabricated package only in the amount of work done at the factory. You cannot really tell the difference between a finished prefab and a modular home once it has been assembled.

Think of a mobile home as a "module," or unit; think of a modular home as two mobile home units joined together at the building site. Actually a modular home is exactly that: two parts of a prebuilt house moved from factory to property and joined there.

As in a mobile home, all work, including interior decoration, is completed at the factory.

Nothing remains to be done but to hook up the electrical facilities and plumbing to the respective utilities—besides, of course, attaching the two modules to the already laid foundation.

FACTORY-ENGINEERED MODULES

Beginning with the floor system, a modular home is engineered at the factory to combine in two halves all the structural, ornamental, and decorative features that are built into conventional houses on the job site.

Complete down to plumbing, electrical systems, painted gypsum walls, installed bathroom fixtures, wall-to-wall carpeting, hard-surface flooring, and installed kitchen cabinets and appliances, the two factory-finished halves are transported by truck to a building site and erected on a completed foundation.

Once the two units are joined together, the roof is constructed by attaching prebuilt panels, and optional panelized garage units and other exterior features can be added with little trouble.

THE LEISURE-HOME MODULE

The modular home concept is ideal for the leisure home, being a double mobile home in actuality, but of course the modular home is more easily adapted to situations where colony-type living is involved.

Modulars are equipped with plumbing facilities, heating facilities, and electrical appliances that depend on attachment to existing sewer systems and electric-power systems. Therefore, if you are planning a house in a retreat far from

This modular home is born in a factory where the floor is built first, with walls added next, as in conventional construction of any shell. Then the roof is attached and the inside roughed-in and finished off. The second step for sectional home comes when it is moved by cab—in two separate sections—from the factory to the building site. The third step is the assembly of the two sections on the building site, when the second section of the house is lowered into place on a foundation that has been built to careful specifications. Section two is then attached to the first section and to foundation, completing assembly. The Sporthaus (below) blends in beautifully with the bucolic atmosphere of the countryside.

any such utilities, it would be best to shop around for a different kind of housing unit.

Westville Homes. One of the modular home builders produces a vacation-style home that has been developed especially for outdoor living. Westville Homes manufactures its vacation home in two sections and hauls them to the site, where they are assembled on a previously prepared foundation.

The builder sends out a work crew to prepare the foundation ahead of time; then another crew follows to set up the sections on the foundation and hook up the utilities.

The house pictured is called The Sporthaus. The floor plan is in the shape of a double-wide mobile home, with a large living room, 24 feet by 11 feet 6 inches, a dining room, 9 feet by 11 feet 6 inches, a kitchen, 10 feet by 11 feet 6 inches, and two bedrooms, the master bedroom 16 feet by 11 feet 6 inches, and the second bedroom 10 feet by 11 feet 6 inches. The front porch measures 23 feet by 7 feet 6 inches. Total living space in The Sporthaus comes to 1,196 square feet, including the front porch. The price of The Sporthaus is $24,000 complete, not including the cost of the lot.

A second model of the same home has slightly smaller rooms, but contains three instead of two bedrooms.

A modular home like this one comes with absolutely everything already furnished for you. All interiors are complete with top-quality merchandise. For instance, in The Sporthaus, Armstrong Calay Cushion Vinyl floors are used, along with top-brand kitchen appliances and bathroom fixtures.

You have the opportunity to select your own colors, patterns, and textures from the brands used, however, so that you can have your choice of floors, walls, and ceilings.

The company can supply extras such as storm windows, shutters, combination storm-and-screen doors, and solid construction at a cost that would be at least 20 percent higher if provided by standard building practices.

In addition, modular construction can save you a great deal of money over which you might otherwise have no control. An absolute cost ceiling is set from the beginning. With conventional building, the cost and time is unpredictable; through factory control, time, quality, and cost can be held to a realistic figure. The time element, also, is considerably shortened in modular construction.

Burkin Homes. A modular-type A-frame is available too—an A-frame vacation chalet developed by Burkin Homes—transportable to any site in North America. Some of these A-frames have been shipped to Alaska.

A folding top enables the house's two halves to be shipped on the highway. When set up on the foundation at the site, the top is folded out and within two days the house is ready for occupancy.

The house, called the Cedar Chalet, comes complete with furniture and all appliances. The exterior design has a rustic finish and a cedar roof and fir plywood siding.

Modular Cedar Chalet starts out in the factory, where two sections of the double-wide, mobile-home-sized pieces are built. Note how roof peaks, which become the top of the A-frame when it is in place on the site, are folded down for shipping by truck. Interior shot of completed home shows a view from the living room toward the dining area. The three floor plans show versatility of the module design, with three different sizes to choose from.

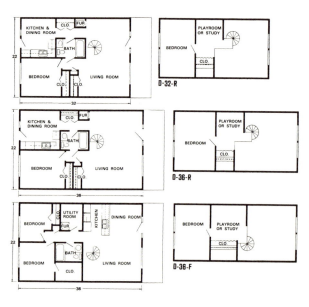

The Cedar Chalet comes in single- and double-wide sizes. The single measures 12 by 36 feet, the double 22 by 38. There are also three lengths: 38, 36, and 32 feet. The cost ranges from $7,000 to $10,000 for a single-wide unit, and from $13,000 to $18,000 for a double-wide one.

The single unit contains two bedrooms, a living room, a kitchen, and a bathroom. The double contains three bedrooms—all large enough for double beds—kitchen, living room, and bath.

The appearance of the modular A-frame is "warm and rustic," in the words of one owner.

MODULAR-HOME INTERIORS

When you buy a modular home, you are buying it complete with all interior decoration. You will not have a shell of a house that you can finish off by yourself, or that you can decorate to your own particular taste. However, because the interior of the average modular home is carefully designed, you will find that you are getting a much better package than you might

A modular home comes already finished, with carpeting as well as wall coverings in place. The living room of this vacation home accentuates the rustic.

The kitchen is bright and airy, with good rugged cushion vinyl floor. The children's room features bunk beds, big windows, and bright colors in the flooring.

conceivably come up with yourself. Also, you will be able to choose from several models, patterns, and colors of most of the interior decorative material. In this way you can exert your individuality on the interior; it is surprising how much variety you can get if you try.

Chapter 8

CUSTOM CONSTRUCTION

IF you have looked over all the plans offered for manufactured vacation homes and still have not found one that you like, you can always resort to the final step: You can hire an architect.

Your idea of a second home may be such that it can only be fulfilled by the special talents of an architect. Or there may be environmental problems at the vacation setting you have chosen for a homesite that can only be solved by a professional engineer. Or your family may have certain demands that necessitate a very special house design that can be provided only by an architect's imagination.

No matter what the reason, you can always call in a professional designer to provide you with the plans for a first-rate second home. He will deliver the plans to you, and when you have

The architect of this low-profiled, sleek, modern beach home has combined the rough stone found in the shore area with the simplicity of plywood construction for this striking custom design. Horizontal lines blend in with flat seascape and far horizon. See interior below.

approved them he will hire a building contractor to do the construction work. As architect, he will supervise erection of the house and make sure the contractor abides by all the stipulations and specifications of the design.

In the long run, you may find that a custom-designed house will give you more for your dollar than a predesigned house supplied by a home manufacturer at a much lower overall price.

Of course, the decision is up to you.

Chimney stone at right of picture repeats texture of rock to which powerboat is tied outside. Sleek wall-beam construction repeats lines of boat.

HOW TO WORK WITH AN ARCHITECT

Construction work, even in its simplest form, can be a complex and baffling puzzle to someone who knows nothing about it. Not only may a cabin put up by an amateur violate building codes he has never heard of, but it may even fall down around his ears.

For the man who has not the time or the skill to build a home himself, yet who wants something a little better than the average packaged home, an architect is the bridge between his dream and reality.

The architect knows how to design a structure that will have maximum strength and durability. He also knows the codes of the community in which he works and so will not violate any laws in planning the house. And he knows enough about the social values of a home to give you the best environment for you and your family.

In working with an architect, here are a few tips that will help you get along with him more easily and so perhaps enable him to design a better house for you.

Family Needs. Every family unit is different from every other family unit. Not only the size of the family, but the individual characteristics of each member differ widely. Each of these many considerations can mean the difference between a home resembling a noisy madhouse full of dissatisfied people and one that is a harmonious, pleasant, and beautiful environment for a happy family.

The first step an architect takes is to acquaint himself with the needs of the people for whom he is working. Be sure that you are frank with him, so that he will know exactly what you like. He is more interested in giving you a pleasant place to live than in providing a snug and efficient "life box."

Here are a few things you should openly discuss with him:

1. *Your pattern of living.* If you are a family of introverts and low-keyed thinkers, you will certainly want a different kind of house from a family of extroverts and party givers. And if your age is in the sixties or seventies, you will live a different life from people in their thirties. The size of your family will suggest a certain type of house to the architect's mind; so will the different ages and occupations and interests of its various members.

2. *Privacy versus gregariousness.* Be particularly honest with your architect about the character makeups of the members of your family. Some people dote on privacy. Others detest it and need people around them at all times. The design of a house can accentuate privacy, or it can accentuate sociability. Be sure you get the right design for *you.*

3. *Dining habits.* Eating—next to sleeping—is one of the most important considerations of any home environment. Tell your architect exactly what you want in the way of dining facilities—how much you need, and if you want a degree of elegance, or mainly efficiency. If you are in the habit of giving parties, you will want a large area in which guests can sit around and eat and chat in comfort. If not, you will want a small, no-fuss eating area.

4. *Sleeping habits.* Man spends one third of his life in bed; be sure that both bed and room

Dramatic setting of rushing stream, heavily wooded terrain, and isolation of woods and mountains add up to the perfect place to build this open, airy, spacious home. The interior of the living room has been laid out with a great deal of lounging area, which can be used for eating and drinking and talking as well as for viewing the surrounding scenery.

are right for you. Some people cannot sleep if there is any light; others, if there is none. Some cannot stand the slightest sound; others cannot sleep unless there is running water nearby, or crashing waves, or traffic noises. If antisound insulation is necessary, be sure to let your architect know about it.

5. *Entertainment.* A gregarious salesman is going to give many more parties than an introverted bank clerk. Your architect should know everything about wanted entertainment areas in your second home: living room; dining room; activities area; outer decks; play room; recreation room; a swimming pool, basketball court, or other sports areas near the house. Also, be sure that there is an allowance for parking space if you expect large groups of people in at one time.

Prepare a Proper Budget. An architect must know how much money you are able to pay for the house. There is no use trying to overstate the amount you think you can pay; the bank will soon disabuse you if you have been too optimistic. On the other hand, do not skimp on an estimated price just because you are tight-fisted. You always get what you pay for; that is, if you cheat here and there, you will not get the good house you want but a second-rate substitute.

Take your architect into your confidence regarding the money you want to spend. Prepare a realistic ceiling price that you can afford, and give this price to the architect. He will use this figure when he is drawing up the plans, giving you the best he can for the amount of money you have indicated you can spend.

If you plan to expand the house later on, when you have some more money available, tell him so. He will design it in such a fashion that rooms can be added to the basic structure. There is nothing more stupid than building a house that fits so snugly on the terrain that you cannot add a room or two later on, particularly if you have had that idea at the back of your mind all the time.

If you simply plan to use this second home for five years and then sell it and buy another, larger one, tell the architect. He will respect your wishes and design the house so that it can be sold to someone else without difficulty.

Do Not Make Changes in Plans. Once you have seen and approved the plans the architect has drawn up for you, do not make any further alterations. He has designed the house with a fixed price in mind.

To make changes after the design has been approved will cost money. If interior walls are shifted about or doors are changed, the whole structure may begin to look unbalanced—physically as well as aesthetically. Changes may necessitate more changes, and then substitutions may have to be made to cut down on the price of some items to remain within the price range you had in mind.

Do Not Use Substitutes for Name Brands. An architect's specifications will always list the quality of each piece of material used. The spec sheet may also indicate a particular brand name.

The brand name of such items as doors, windows, bathroom fixtures, and the like is a most important quality control for you. A floor board of a particular brand is known for its reliability, its durability, its beauty, and its overall excellence; that is why that brand-name item costs more.

To substitute something else for a brand-name item is a favorite cost-cutting device used by fly-by-night builders. An architect will not allow substitutes of this kind. If you find too many repetitions of the phrase "or equal" in the specifications, talk to your architect to see why he is using it. For instance, if you find the phrase "Masonite interior paneling, or equal" or "Armstrong tile, or equal"—look out. Ask the architect why he has allowed for substitution.

On the other hand, a second home is not a first home. It does not need the same intricate trim and expensive millwork. The architect can cut back on these foofaraws and bring the price down when you remind him that you do not want all those costly little extras.

In other words: Cut down on the jazzy gimcrackery; but do not use substitutes for brand names in vital materials.

ARCHITECT AND CONTRACTOR

An architect usually hires a contractor with whom he is familiar to construct the house he has designed. It is not a good idea for you as owner to insist on using some contractor whom the architect does not know. For good teamwork, architect and contractor must mesh well, like the cogs in a smooth-running machine. If there is conflict between them, your house will suffer.

Do not keep running over to the house site

every day or two to check up on the progress of the work. Very likely you will not see the contractor anyway. Workers on the site take their orders from their boss, not from you. Nor should they take orders from you. Do not assume the authority of the contractor at any time; it will cost you money.

The contractor is actually the builder of the house. It is his job to hire all carpenters and laborers to put up the foundation, floor, walls, and roof. The contractor then hires subcontractors—plumbers, electricians, heating men, painters—to put in pipes, wiring, heat, and apply paint. Subcontractors are responsible to the contractor. Do not interfere in the working relationship between the contractor and his subcontractors.

Interesting modern adaptation of ancient windmill combined with modern lighthouse shows skillful use of plywood in seaside construction. Surface of home is allowed to weather in stiff sea breezes and salt air. Opposite: Windows are portholes to emulate seafaring vessels. Bed is even hung by chains from boxed beams in imitation of a sailor's hammock.

All About Time. An architect's time is budgeted. He must spend a great deal of time on a large building project, like an apartment building, or a school. But he can allot only a limited amount of time to a small job like a second home.

On the average, you will probably have three or four interviews with the architect before the plans are approved. He will then go to the site three or four times to supervise the construction and see that the building contractor has followed his plans and used only the brands mentioned on the specification sheets.

Do not make endless phone calls to the architect with minor complaints. Do not involve yourself in endless recriminations about a small item that turns out not to be what you really wanted. Let it pass.

In short, treat your architect as you would a business associate who is there to help you. If you treat him in that fashion, he will do all in his power to give you the best house for the money.

HOW TO WORK WITH A CONTRACTOR

While the architect is the man who puts the dream of a house on paper, the contractor is the man who translates the plans of the architect into physical reality. As has been partially explained, he hires carpenters, laborers, and subcontractors, buys material for all phases of the construction, and keeps the men at work on the building site. In construction terms, the contractor *is* the "builder."

An architect can work in conjunction with a contractor; he can hire a contractor to put up a house he has planned, as we have discussed

Triple-Threat Tri-Level is intended for construction on a sloping terrain, but can be erected on flat land. This is one of a series of available leisure-home plans conforming to uniform building codes. The 36-by-50-foot structure has three levels, with several design options offered for the upper story. Use of such a predesigned set of plans eliminates the necessity to hire an architect for this 1,184–1,216-square-foot house.

before; or he can actually work *for* a building contractor who has hired him to design a certain type of structure.

It is possible for you to secure a set of working plans for a leisure home from a service specializing in vacation home plans, like the Home Building Plan Service. If this case, you do not hire an architect, but go directly to a contractor with the plans you have purchased and hire him to put up the design you have selected.

There are in this chapter several homes built from "stock" plans which you can buy. The homes on pages 147, 154, and 155 in this chapter have been designed by architects working for the Western Wood Products Association. The plans in Chapter Two have been designed by architects working for the American Plywood Association. The addresses of these organizations and others specializing in the sale of carefully designed plans, which can be followed by professional builders anywhere, appear after the last chapter of this book under the section heading "Second Home Plans." The cost of a set of plans is nominal, but remember that a good set of working drawings and specifications may cost from $35 to $50, since they contain the very detailed information that a contractor must have.

In hiring a contractor and in working with him to build a house, there are some things you should keep in mind about the relationship between homeowner and contractor/builder in order to get the best work possible from him.

Getting the Right Contractor Builder. There are all kinds of builders and contractors, as a glance at the yellow pages of the telephone book will indicate. Selecting the right one can be a problem, although not an insurmountable one.

Here are some points to remember in your hunt for the right contractor:

1. *Reputation.* Most building contractors come to be known for the quality of the work they do, good or bad. You can usually ask around among your friends to find out who is a good contractor and who among them has a less-than-favorable reputation.

2. *Financial standing.* A contractor is responsible for hiring workmen and buying material. If his financial standing is shaky, there may be delays in putting up your house. The contractor you hire should have a good financial standing; a call to the bank that finances him should give you the proper information to proceed.

3. *References.* Most contractors have a file of references they have collected through the years. Check these over and then go and look at the houses indicated. You will be able to find out more about the contractor in this way than in any other. Talk to the people living in houses he has built.

4. *Second-home skills.* Be sure the man you want to build your second home is familiar with this type of construction. A contractor who has made a good name for himself putting up drugstores will not necessarily put up a good vacation house. Likewise, a man who puts up excellent beach houses may not do very well with a mountain home on a steep, rocky slope. Be sure that the contractor you hire knows how to put up what you want him to put up.

Terms of Payment. It is extremely important

that the exact amounts of money owed to the contractor be spelled out and put in writing before any money changes hands. Be sure that you know not only the amount of each payment you are to make and when you have to make it, but exactly where every penny is going.

The typical builder's agreement usually involves certain portions of the total payment at certain stages of construction.

For instance: the first 20 percent is due after the foundation has been laid; another 20 percent when the shell has been erected; 20 percent more when the subcontractors are through with their work; 20 percent when the plasterers, painters, and finishers are through; and a final 20 percent upon completion of the final inspection of the house.

Be sure that such a contract is carefully drawn up and that you know exactly how much work is supposed to have been done when you pay each amount. A mix-up in timing can not only delay you indefinitely, but can throw the contractor into a situation where his own payments for materials are delayed; such a postponement can jeopardize workmen and suppliers in the next step of construction.

Contractual Agreement. When dealing with a building contractor, keep all lines of communication open—in both directions. If you have a complaint, you should be able to reach him to voice it. If he has some questions, or a decision has to be made, he should be able to reach you. In this way, differences of opinion can be ironed out in an amicable way before they snowball into real obstacles.

The contract you sign with the builder must be complete and airtight. It should also be clear to you exactly what you are getting at each step of the operation. The average contract should include all of the following in detail:

1. *Architect's plans.* The plans used must be working drawings, elevations, and all construction details that might raise questions in the mind of the average workman. Stock plans purchased from services are usually clear enough and specific enough to give good working instructions to all building tradesmen. The contractor should stick to the plans and make his subcontractors toe the line. You must know exactly what the plan shows in order to follow through the steps yourself.

2. *Specifications.* Every house plan is accompanied by a set of specifications, in which are detailed the kind of wood to be used, the size of structure timber, the brand of certain appliances, the types of wood, metal, and other construction materials used, the brand, type, and color of paint, and so on. The contractor should not make substitutions in this list unless you agree to the changes.

3. *Lawyer.* In drawing up a contractual agreement between you and the contractor, you should hire a lawyer to supervise the writing, checking, and signing of the agreement. Only in this way do you have legal recourse to demand changes in the construction of the house if it deviates from the plans and specifications.

During Construction. Once the agreement has been signed, the contractor begins to build the house as specified in the working drawings and the spec sheets. You will be able to select the exact type of building supplies: doors, windows, cabinets, hardware, and so on. Builders have catalogs in which the material is listed and specified by name and number. Be sure to see that the item you check off is actually installed by the builder.

If there are any requests for substitutions because of shortages of certain materials, you and the contractor must agree on the particular item to be substituted. This agreement should be in writing to avoid future conflict.

Any other situations involving special equipment, or the use of unusual types of construction, should be written out clearly and agreed to by all concerned. During construction, you should make sure these procedures are taking place as specified.

However, as mentioned before, do not haunt the building site and ask questions of the workmen. A tradesman is hired by the contractor and is responsible for doing the job the contractor has told him to do. If you see something wrong, speak to the contractor directly and come to some kind of understanding with him.

About Subcontractors. If you have hired a contractor to put up your house, he will in turn hire plumbers, electricians, and heating experts to subcontract these items. Do not interfere with the contractor's choice in these subcontracting situations.

Final Inspection. When the contractor tells you that he has finished the house, you will inspect the entire structure carefully. Be sure to note anything that might be the slightest bit out of line—inferior brands substituted for name brands, unfinished molding, or sloppy paint application.

Make a list of everything that you think is not up to par, and present the list to the building contractor. Be sure that you have written down everything you want fixed. It is a good idea to send this list of complaints in the form of a letter; then, when the contractor has corrected the faults, he will respond with a letter of his own.

At that point, reinspect the property and see that all your complaints have been taken care of. Then write another stating that you have found everything satisfactory and ready for occupancy.

Be sure that all your complaints have been taken care of. Do not settle your debt to the contractor until everything is exactly the way you want it.

Utilities. At this point the builder will bring in subcontractors once again to hook up gas pipes, electric wiring, and water pipes to the proper utility connections.

The contractor will turn over to you warranties and instruction manuals for all mechanical equipment. You should fill out all these yourself and send them in to the manufacturers for your protection.

Final Settlement. Now is the time to pay the last portion of the money. When you hand the check over, the contractor has fulfilled his obligations and has no legal obligation to the property.

H-shaped house shown in two different versions demonstrates versatility of architectural plan. The main difference lies in the position of the fireplace. Left-hand plan is designed for cooler, desert, or plateau regions, where the winds blow hard at night and the day's warmth vanishes when the sun goes down. There's plenty of glass to enjoy that fantastic desert or foothills view. Right-hand plan (opposite) is intended for use in the more moderate climatic conditions of the range country. Here the ranch elements of the design predominate.

According to the law, once settlement is made and you move into the house, the property is your own responsibility. In other words, when you take possession of the house, you cannot force the builder to do any more work for you, even though you might suddenly discover some glaring error that you had not noticed before.

Getting Along with the Contractor. Treat the contractor exactly as you would treat an architect—with consideration, firmness, and understanding. If you do, he will deliver to you the best house he can provide.

How to Deal with a Subcontractor. The subcontractor's job is not quite so complex or wide-ranging as the building contractor's. He is a tradesman with a specific skill—plumbing, electrical work, installing the heating plant, or painting.

When the subcontractor is hired by the contractor, you will have little to do with him, except see the end result of his work. However, in the case of a shell prefab you have put up yourself, or a precut package at the shell stage, you may have to hire your own subcontractor to do the job for you.

Show him the plans of the house and let him figure out how he will rough in the pipes or the electric wiring, and then get an estimate from him. If the estimate is too high, talk with him and try to figure out how you can cut the price.

Once you have decided on a price, be sure that all the brands in the specifications, or that you have decided on in your discussions with him, are included in the agreement. Then let him go ahead.

When he is finished, check the results, and if you are dissatisfied, tell him why. Once he has fixed whatever is wrong, you should then inspect the installation again, send him a letter of satisfaction, and pay him off.

Be sure that everything has been corrected to your satisfaction before you make out a check to him. Once he has been paid, he no longer has any responsibility to the job.

Treat a subcontractor exactly as you would an architect or a building contractor: You are paying him to do a job, and you must be firm with him, but also considerate and understanding.

Chapter 9

BUILDING TIPS

Although the principal steps in construction have already been touched on in the preceding chapters, it is a good idea to familiarize yourself with them if you are doing any of the work on your second home yourself, or even if you are having someone else do it for you.

The brief outline below does not include some of the more intricate steps in carpentry or roughing-in, but it does give you a more or less standard step-by-step procedure in the construction of any house.

1. Foundation
2. Shell
   a. Floor
   b. Walls
   c. Roof
   d. Doors and windows

3. Roughing-in
   a. Electricity
   b. Plumbing
   c. Heating
   d. Masonry
4. Finishing off
   a. Paneling
   b. Flooring
   c. Millwork
   d. Painting
5. Utilities
6. Appliances
7. Landscaping

FOUNDATION

If you are about to erect the shell of a second home, you will first have to make provisions for the foundation on which the shell is to be placed.

There are several types of foundations to choose from: wooden posts, stones, concrete piers, or continuous concrete.

Wooden Posts. Although they are not actually recommended by all building experts today, wooden posts can be used to support small cabins. The best kinds of wood to use for such posts are cedar, cypress heartwood, locust, and redwood. All other woods must be treated with chlorophenol or zinc naphthenate in order to make them resistant to exposure.

Ordinary wood, the least dense of all foundation materials, tends to disintegrate faster than other foundation materials, and unfortunately it is also susceptible to rot, insect attack, and many other ills. The four woods mentioned have a high resin content and are tightly grained, which is the reason they are resistant to decay and insect attack.

Wooden posts must be about a foot in diameter, and they should be long enough to extend below the frost line in cold areas and down to solid rock or dense gravel in unstable ground.

For a sandy beach site, wooden posts are usually the most practical material for a foundation. Such posts should be pressure-treated, impregnated with creosote, and then sunk into the earth like a wharf piling.

Stones. Rock can be used to good advantage either as a foundation support or as the foundation itself. Lay two large, flat boulders one on top the other to form a common and serviceable support. The reason for using two stones is to keep ground moisture from rising past them into the wood timbers supporting the floor. Do not cement the stones together; the air space between them traps the moisture.

The two rocks should fit firmly and evenly so that they do not slip or shift under the weight of the structure atop them.

Rock supports work best on a site where the cabin rests on solid or nearly solid rock. In dirt or gravel, it is necessary to dig down to solid rock or to very firm gravel to lay the boulders; then concrete piers must be used to raise the floor to grade level.

Concrete Piers. A most common foundation support used in vacation homes is a series of concrete piers. There are many ways these piers can be formed. Wooden, metal, or even building-paper forms are available commercially. By pouring wet concrete aggregate into the form, a pier of the exact size and shape needed can be made.

Precast piers are also available, but these are sometimes difficult to haul in from great distances. However, they are inexpensive and adequate for easily accessible places.

In using concrete piers, consult an engineer, or use a plan provided by an architect or plan service, so that the piers are placed in the right spots to support the carrying members of the house.

If you do not find a conventional shape that suits your project, you can cast your own piers in cylindrical shape, or in cones of your own design. Concrete can be dyed, so that these foundation piers—if visible—will blend in with the rest of the house and terrain.

In cold areas, make sure that the piers extend below the frost line. Otherwise they may be tilted out of true in a rapid freeze-thaw shift in weather. No matter what your locality is, make sure that the concrete piers rest on a solid support.

The advantage of concrete piers is that they promote needed ventilation under the house. The disadvantage is that they do not keep out pests and rodent life.

Continuous Concrete. Generally speaking continuous concrete all around the perimeter of a house makes the most satisfactory and permanent type of foundation. The weight of the entire structure is best distributed this way, and there is less chance of any settling or sinking of the house.

In many vacation areas, sand and gravel are available; a concrete foundation is most practical in such a spot.

A continuous concrete foundation should normally be twice as wide as the width of the finished wall of a wood-frame dwelling. This rule of thumb applies to most solid-ground situations. In marshy and boggy or unstable soil, the foundation footing should be still wider.

Actually, the width of the foundation may vary according to the weight that has to be supported. If you are using logs or timbers, the foundation should be at least two inches thicker than the logs.

In some vacation areas, you can purchase at a nominal cost premixed concrete aggregate for use as foundation material.

SHELL

The shell of any house includes the floor, the walls, and the roof. The hanging of doors and windows is usually considered a part of the shell.

Floor. Roughly two types of floors can be considered practical for a second home: a concrete slab floor and a wooden floor.

Concrete Slab. In some areas it is practically impossible to lay a concrete slab floor. If the site is some distance from a good access road, it will be most difficult to haul in concrete and sand.

A slab floor has a number of advantages:

1. It is the best surface on which to lay flagstones, brick, linoleum, or a tile floor.

2. A slab floor keeps the profile of the house close to the ground, giving it a pleasing line in relation to the landscape.

3. A slab is easier to clean than a wood floor.

4. It is free of rodents.

But a slab floor also has disadvantages:

1. The cost of transporting cement may be too high.

2. In areas where the ground freezes, the slab may buckle and disintegrate under the constant expansion and contraction of the earth.

3. A slab may break up in unstable soils and in adobe.

4. Excavation for the slab may cost too much.

NOTE: Pouring concrete is a difficult undertaking for the rank amateur. It is a good idea to have help unless you are experienced in concrete work.

Wood Floor. There are several advantages to the average wooden floor in a second home:

1. A wood floor is generally warmer than a concrete slab because wood is a less effective heat conductor.

2. A wood floor blends in better than any other kind with log- or rough-textured cabin construction.

3. It is much simpler to build a wood floor than it is to pour concrete.

Generally speaking, a wood floor can be made of almost any rough-finished lumber. Tongue-and-groove 2-by-6 boards make a fine weather-tight decking. This type of flooring can be used without subflooring.

The conventional wood flooring in the average

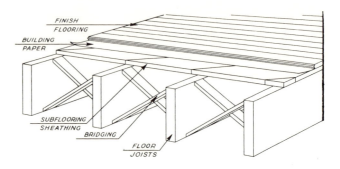

home is composed of strip wood flooring over a subflooring of sheathing. The illustration accompanying shows how it is installed. The subflooring can be strip sheathing laid at a diagonal to the joists, or it can be plywood sheets. The bridging X's between the floor joists are a common structural precaution to keep the joists on a vertical plane.

Observe the sheet of building paper between subflooring and finish flooring. It is used for insulation and to cut down frictional creaking between flooring and sheathing.

Strip flooring is nailed at frequent intervals along its length and when properly put down is practically indestructible. The flooring strips are tongue-and-grooved for a tight fit.

A form of strip flooring that is excellent for vacation homes is a modern version of the old plank flooring seen in early American houses. Wood dowel pegs are simulated in some of these floors. This type of flooring comes in random widths to recapture the appearance of pre-Colonial floors.

Block flooring—a type of parquet—comes in nine-inch squares. Laminated hardwood blocks are also available.

One of the best, simplest, and strongest floors

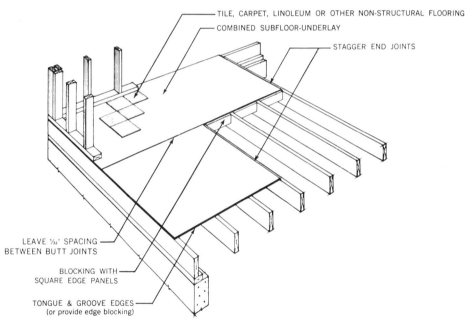

is a combination subfloor-underlayment made of one thickness of plywood. The illustration accompanying shows a typical plywood floor.

Walls. Although many different kinds of

building materials can be used for the walls of a house, they tend to separate into two basic types: Masonry, such as stone, concrete, or aggregate blocks; and wood, such as logs, crib planks, or conventional wood-frame construction.

Masonry. Laying masonry is a difficult task, but if you are up to it, stone walls make a fine house that is impervious to fire, weather, and rats. But a wall of stone requires a heavier foundation than a wall of wood.

Stone Construction. A stone wall should be 18 inches thick at the bottom and then taper to 8 inches at the top, far wider than the ordinary wood-frame wall. Because of the thickness of the wall at its base, the foundation supporting it has to be 20 inches wide.

Uncut stones are called rubble; cut stones, ashlar. Ashlar work is expensive. Most stone cabins are made of uncut rock grouted together with ordinary mortar.

To build a stone wall, clean each stone, soak it in water, and then lay it in mortar, using mortar freely to give each new stone plenty of support and purchase to those next to it.

Concrete or Aggregate-Block Construction. Concrete blocks or bricks are usually easier to use than stones. Concrete blocks come in many sizes, although the most common is 8 by 8 by 16 inches. For a concrete-block wall, a heavy footing equivalent to that used with a stone wall is required. Concrete blocks are laid just like bricks, with mortar applied between and underneath them to give support and to bind the blocks together.

Log Construction. Chapter Four has already dealt with the use of prepared logs for cabins. If you want to make your own logs, you can always follow the general rules of commercial manufacturers.

You can lay the logs horizonatally, or you can lay them vertically in what is called stockade construction. But, frankly, it is much easier to use precut logs as described in Chapter Four.

Crib Construction. You can lay 2-by-4 or 2-by-6 milled lumber face to face, with each "course" nailed securely to the one below for a type of building called crib construction. The corners are crosslapped, with the resulting walls strong and fire-resistant because there is no air between timbers to feed the flames. The illustration shows how each corner appears.

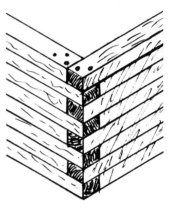

As with a log cabin, no vertical framing is needed. The surface facing inside the house is the finished wall, as in real log-cabin structure. You can use mill ends and other odd lengths of low-grade, low-cost lumber for material.

Wood-Frame Construction. The greatest advantage of wood-frame construction is its versatility and simplicity. The typical wood-frame wall is simply composed of studs sheathed and sided with one of several types of wooden material.

The schematic diagram shown illustrates methods of partition construction. The basic procedure in the building of any wood-frame wall is to construct it on the floor, flat down,

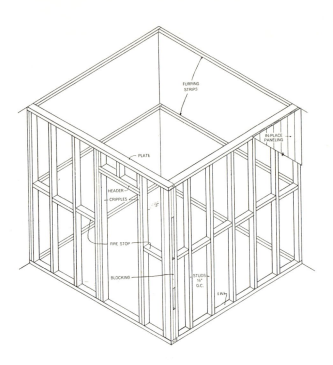

and then raise it into place and fasten it to the adjacent wall running at right angles to it.

To build a partition, you should know the terms illustrated in the drawing. The bottom horizontal 2-by-4 is the sill; the top one, the plate. The upright that connects them is the stud.

To proceed, lay the sill 2-by-4 on its edge and nail a stud to it, with the end at right angles to the sill. Use two 16-penny nails through the sill. Lay the plate against the stud and nail it in place in a similar manner. Continue nailing studs between sill and plate exactly 16 inches on center—each center 16 inches from the next center.

Horizontally, and midway between the sill and the plate, nail another horizontal 2-by-4. This is called the fire stop. Stagger adjacent fire stops so you can nail through studs without having to toenail, or nail in at a diagonal angle.

Where a door is wanted, nail the frame from a prehung door in place and build a double-frame around it.

Then, with one person at each end of the partition, lift the entire wall in place. Be sure the partition is at right angles to another wall before fastening it to the floor. Fasten the sill to the foundation by means of a bolt drilled into the concrete. Check to see that the partition is absolutely vertical before fastening it to the wall at right angles to it.

So much for the partition itself—that is, the bare bones of the wall. To be finished off, both sides of the partition must be covered. To complete the shell, only the outer portion of the exterior partition need be applied.

For siding, which is what the outer surface of a house is called, you can use a large variety of materials to cover the studding: unfinished lumber, milled sidings of all varieties, shingles and shakes, plywood, and specialty sidings.

Unfinished Lumber. This can be applied in board-and-batten fashion or lapped, making a serviceable and rugged rustic wall. Board and batten is the easier of the two for the amateur to handle.

First, nail the broad boards in a vertical position. Then nail a strip of batten flat over each joint between the boards. You can lap the rough boards horizonatally, shingle-fashion, too, if you want.

Milled Siding. There are over two hundred different styles and sizes of wood siding available

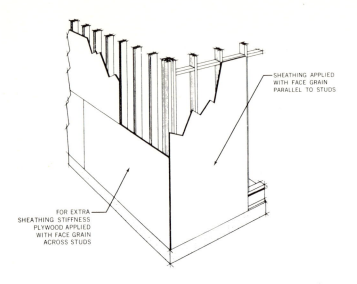

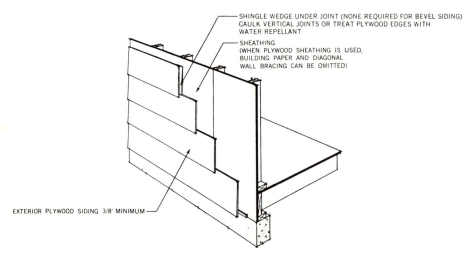

to the builder today. You can lap these sidings either over strip sheathing or over plywood-sheet sheathing. The illustrations show some typical exterior applications.

The first demonstrates how to apply plywood sheets only; such a surface can be used as an excellent base for a good paint job.

The second illustrates how to apply lap-siding strips horizontally over a plywood-sheathing surface.

Shingles and Shakes. Western cedar, redwood, and cypress shingles and shakes do very well for exterior wall surfaces of beach or mountain cabins. Apply shingles in a manner similar to the application of horizontal sheathing as illustrated in the second drawing above.

Plywood. A number of plywood exteriors have been developed for use on vacation homes. Photographs of them and other pertinent information appear in Chapter Two on materials.

The third illustration shows the application of Texture 1-11 exterior panel siding to plywood sheathing.

Since plywood surfaces, including all edges, should be thoroughly primed, sealed, and painted, be sure to study the section on painting plywood—interior and exterior—in Chapter Eleven.

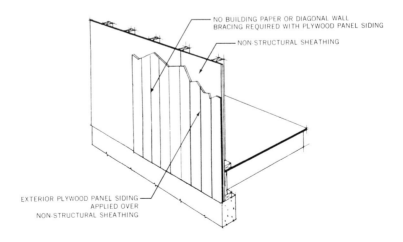

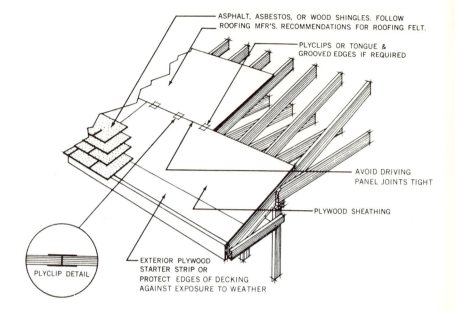

Roof. Most cabin roofs are surfaced with shingles or shakes, or even with regular roofing paper applied directly over plywood sheathing.

In warm climates reflective roofing material can be used to control the temperature inside the cabin itself, such as crushed dolomite over built-up tar and gravel, or even brightly painted canvas.

In heavy-snow areas, you must give extra strength to the roof. Metal shingles provide adequate strength; so do sheet-metal strips.

Study the illustration of a typical roofing installation for suggestions as to the proper components for a conventional roof.

Doors. The last step in completing the shell of a structure is the hanging of doors and windows.

The frames of both doors and windows are

built into the walls; see the section on partition construction for an explanation. The actual doors and windows are built into these frames, the doors hung on hinges, and the windows simply attached to the studs, since the frames usually come with the entire window unit.

A good door is equivalent to a good piece of furniture. It lends character to a room and carries out the design theme of the front of the house right through the interior.

Because a door can add so much to a room or an entrance, its appearance is a primary consideration. There are two kinds of doors you can choose from—flush doors and panel doors. Flush Doors are hollow inside and have no surface design. Panel Doors have carefully ensculptured pieces and are joined to form imaginative designs.

For exterior doors, you can choose designs that reflect various modes of architecture, such as Colonial, Traditional, or Contemporary style.

Colonial Door. For the front door of the house, a door of Colonial design might be a good choice, depending on the architecture of the rest of the exterior. Colonial is a modification of classic, with the Greek columns suggested in the side panels and the pediment reproduced as a decorative feature above.

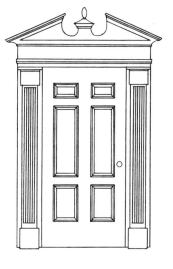

Traditional Door. The Traditional door is a modification of the classic or Colonial door, with panels at the sides and top. The door itself is the same in both Colonial and Traditional style; only the panels are different. The patterns in the door itself can be altered by using panels that may be square, rectangular, or even slightly curved.

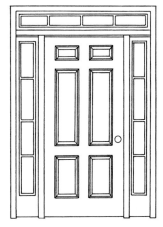

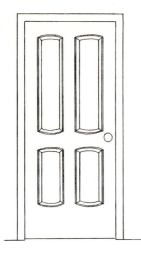

Contemporary Door. The Contemporary door is usually simpler than the more old-fashioned type. There are no side or top panels. Designs can be cut into the face of the door either in slightly rounded patterns or in rectangular or square shapes. This simple design will blend in with almost any type of house style.

For interior doors, you can choose doors that slide, doors that fold, combination doors, Dutch doors, and patio doors.

Sliding Doors. These can be used where space is a real problem. They are perfect for dining rooms, bedrooms, family rooms, and closets.

Folding Doors. They can separate one room from another without taking up much space. They are fine for closets, too, because they are easy to open and close.

Dutch Doors. With the top half open, you can keep children in and stray animals out and enjoy the inside of the house and the outdoors at the same time.

Sliding Door

Folding Door

Dutch Door

Combination Doors. A combination door is a storm/screen door placed in front of the regular door, the storm door in winter, the screen door in summer. Its function is to keep out cold and rain in winter and let in a breeze in the summer.

Combination Door

Patio Door

Patio Doors. These keep either the cold or the heat out. These sliding doors are best when they are dual-glazed—they consist of two pieces of glass with a layer of insulating air sandwiched between them.

Windows. The beauty, livability, and comfort of your home is in a great degree dependent on the windows you have. Take a look at the various kinds you can use.

Double-Hung Wood Window. The double-hung consists of two sashes which slide silently up and down in channels in the frame. This is the conventional all-purpose window used in

Double hung wood window

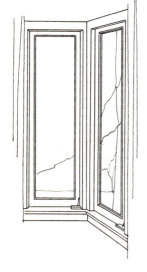

Casement window

more than half the homes of this country. The double-hung blends with Colonial and Traditional architecture. Yet your house can also get a modern look with a double-hung window with horizontal muntin bars. Study the drawing on this page.

Casement Window. The casement is a sash window hinged at the side which you swing outward by means of a crank or lever. It is an easy window to open and close. You can clean the casement from inside, and it is weathertight against dust, drafts, and heat. Wood casements are perfect in kitchens, over the sink or the counter and other hard-to-reach places because the crank can be operated with one wrist motion.

Sliding Windows. Two sashes slide horizontally, right or left, in a common frame, permitting maximum visibility. Sliding windows can give you a sweeping view of the terrain and are therefore perfect for leisure or second homes where scenery is at its best. These windows are trim, neat, and ideal in a living or dining room, too.

Sliding window

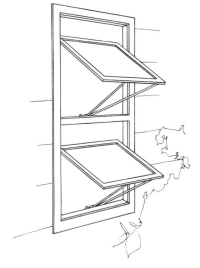

Awning Window

Awning Window. Normally, you can swing the sections of this versatile window up and down, but they can also swing in and down. You can even turn an awning window on its side and use it as a casement. Such flexibility makes this window easy to ventilate; it can be opened fully or at any angle for air control, and it can be left open in all but a driving rain. Modern homes use awning windows because they suit the simple and predominantly horizontal lines of modern architecture; they are perfect for ranch-type houses and second homes.

Bow and Bay Window. The bow window curves out, and the bay is straight in the center and angled at each end. Both windows date from Colonial days and are now available as precision-built preassembled units. Good for Georgian or Colonial-style houses, these windows break up the stiff conventional rectangular lines of a house.

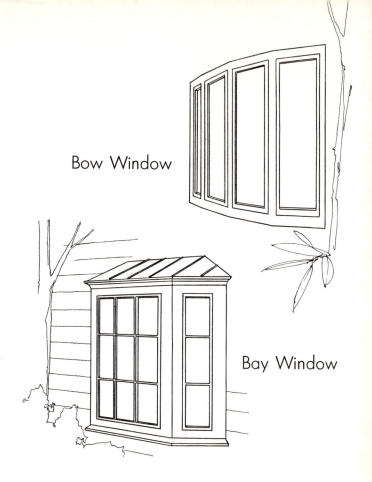

Bow Window

Bay Window

ROUGHING-IN

Roughing-in includes the steps accomplished by subcontractors who handle plumbing, electric wiring, heating, and masonry.

Although you might be able to handle some of this work even though you are an amateur, it is not advisable to try any of these specialities if you know nothing about them.

For all such highly technical work, hire a professional tradesman. It will pay you in the end.

FINISHING OFF

The finishing off of the house includes the application of the final surface to all walls and ceiling, the application of the finish surface to all floors, and the installation of all millwork, including molding. It also includes the installation of all built-in furniture—shelves, cupboards, closet fittings, and the like—all that is generally called millwork.

Paneling. The vacation home is the place for the use of wood paneling. There are two kinds of paneling: traditional paneling formed by individual tongue-and-groove boards, and plywood paneling that has been finished off at the factory before installation.

Traditional Paneling. The drawn illustrations offer some suggestions for special designs in traditional wood paneling: random-width horizontal paneling, vertical paneling, combined horizontal and vertical paneling, herringbone, and wainscoting.

Plywood Paneling. Interior plywood paneling comes in 4-by-8-foot modules, which can be installed either by nailing them directly on to the studs or by adhesive application to another surface. Plywood paneling is an extremely simple method of finishing off, and it will give you a permanent surface in minutes. You simply add molding at the top and bottom when you are finished.

Flooring. There are many different kinds of finish flooring possible including tile, strip wood, linoleum, and tongue-and-groove hardwood.

You can lay flooring yourself without too much difficulty. Attach it to the subflooring that has been supplied in the shell stage of the house. See Chapter Twelve on Interior Decoration for types of flooring.

Millwork. Millwork includes trim and built-in furniture.

Trim. The most common type of trim in a house is molding, a wood embellishment that covers defects in joints and adds a kind of elegance to an otherwise bare wall surface.

There are five basic kinds of molding:

Casing is used in every room of the house. It completes the trimming of doors, windows, and other openings. It may also be used for cabinet trim and certain decorative effects. The drawing shows four kinds of typical casing. Note the hollow back—the recess in the middle of the back—which enables the molding to fit snugly on any wall surface.

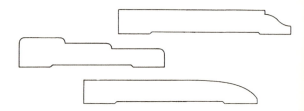

Baseboard is used in every room, too. It runs along the bottom of the wall at its junction with the flooring. It protects the wall bottom from everyday wear and tear. Use a "base shoe" or "quarter round" molding to complete the trim. See this item separately under "Miscellaneous" below.

Cornice is also used in every room. It softens the lines where two planes meet, usually wall and ceiling. Cornice stretches across two right-angle surfaces, usually in a diagonal line. It can trim beams and exterior overhangs. Alone, or in combination with other moldings, cornice molding is used to decorate mantels and picture frames.

Wainscot Caps are used in any room where wainscot paneling—paneling reaching up to about waist height—occurs. Some patterns have a wraparound tip to conceal craftsmanship defects. Others may be used to cap baseboards.

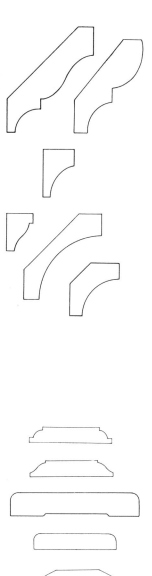

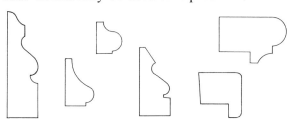

Chair Rail is used for dining rooms, playrooms, and other areas subject to chair-back damage. It should be the proper height, depending on furniture style: older chair backs stand about 36 inches high; modern chairs tend to be several inches lower. Chair rail protects the walls from scratches.

Miscellaneous Trim. All these types of stock are used for various purposes. Quarter rounds, also called base shoe moldings, are used in conjunction with other types of molding. Picture molding is used for framing paintings and photographs. Corner guards are used where two walls meet, forming an outer angle open to frequent damage. Battens are used for board-and-batten combinations. Handrails are used for

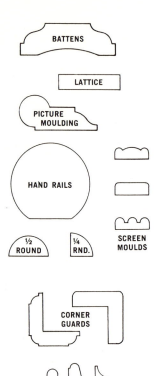

stairs, and closet rods for clothes closets.

Built-Ins. The last carpentry step in finishing off is the construction of built-in furnishings—shelves, cupboards, special closets, cabinets, and the like. Refer to Chapter Twelve for instructions, diagrams, and typical installations in vacation houses.

Painting. Painting is a most important step in the final decoration of any house. Chapter Eleven discusses the application of paint.

Utilities. The utilities are hooked up by the subcontractors responsible for putting in the pipes and electric wires.

Appliances. Appliances, like refrigerators, stoves, and heaters, are delivered and hooked up to the existing utility outlets.

Landscaping. After the house is finished, the area around it is landscaped. Decoration of an entire building site is discussed in Chapter Sixteen.

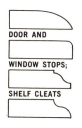

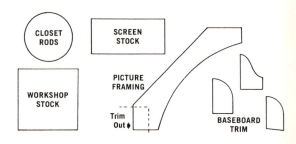

Chapter 10

DESIGNS AND STYLES

THERE are literally dozens of different designs and styles of vacation homes from which you can choose. Through the pages of this book you have already met many of them, either as pure examples of their style or as modifications.

When deciding on a design and style for your vacation home, you can always base your own conception on a conventional plan, and then make your own variation of it.

Design refers to the shape, size, and general look of the house; style refers to the architectural mood conveyed by the windows, doors, siding, and the materials used.

For instance, take the A-frame. This very, very old basic design—seen in the teepee as well as in the ski-and-snow home—is designed to shed snow and ice as well as to withstand wind and rain, all through the use of geometry's most efficient structure, the triangle.

The Swiss chalet, although not an A-frame at all, resembles it because it, too, employs the steeply sloping roof to shed snow and ice so that the structure does not cave in under tons of precipitation.

In fact, the peaked roof is used in many other woods and mountain homes. The typical peaked-roof vacation home designed for the woods is usually called a lodge, which is the word the Indians used to describe a wigwam or teepee.

The style of the mountain lodge varies greatly in the United States. And though a lodge near a lake might well be designed exactly like a lodge in the woods, two lodges in the same woods might be *styled* differently, one constructed of real logs, and the other of wood-frame construction sided with rough-sawn redwood.

For the seashore, a Cape Cod home might be styled in bleached cedar shakes to give it the appearance of an old seaside dwelling. On the other hand, a Cap Cod house away from the shore might be sided with plywood Exterior 1-11 in a cedar finish, or in rough-sawn southern pine.

Again, the Colonial saltbox design immediately brings to mind the sea; a saltbox in unpainted shakes or weathered clapboard fits nicely into a shore locale. Yet a saltbox in brightly painted plywood panels can give a mountainside retreat exactly the right look and present a totally different aspect.

A ranch house can be built of ordinary horizontal siding, yet using that basic design and siding it with vertical board and batten gives the ranch house an entirely different appeal.

The idea is to try to acquaint yourself with all the nuances of design and style that are offered on the vacation-house market.

Architects use the word "style" to indicate certain visual effects. The terms "traditional style," "contemporary style," "Colonial style," "Cape Cod style," and "ranch style" immediately bring to mind a specific kind of house, with recognized design *and* style.

The word "ranch house" suggests a long, low, and flat house in design, and an exterior of textured wood with contemporary doors and windows.

The word "Cape Cod" suggests a house that is a cottage in design, with traditional windows and doors.

These particular words are architectural shorthand and refer to specific designs, styles, and types of houses. Generally speaking, however, design gives you the silhouette and the broad outer lines; style gives you the siding, the kind of door, the shape of window, and the type of roofing.

A house of extremely modern lines, with bold, flat, sharp angles, can be made even more modern by using a lot of glass and rough-sawn beams. But combine bold modern lines with vertical knotty-cedar exterior siding, and you achieve an entirely different look.

Cabin designs are limitless. So are variations in siding surfaces. Thorough knowledge of the various types of siding, interior paneling, and roofing available will allow you to plan your own individual house within the limits of conventional design and style.

EXTERIOR STYLING

A relatively small number of vacation homes are built of stone, brick, or masonry; the majority are made of conventional wood-frame construction, with some kind of wood used for the outer surface in the form of lap siding, shingles, hardboard, or textured plywood.

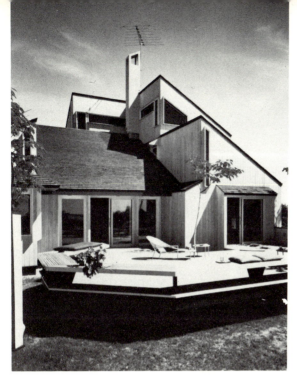

Note how the judicious use of vertical siding can give an entirely different look to three types of vacation houses. The lakeside home (opposite top) becomes almost rustic in appearance, with the vertical lines reminiscent of an old barn siding. The snow-and-ski house (opposite bottom), has, on the contrary, an extremely modern look in its utilitarian simplicity, with 8-inch reverse board-and-batten redwood giving a rugged mountain flavor to the exterior. The plains house on Long Island (above) becomes a contemporary version of a medieval castle, with steep slopes like towers and the siding dominated by big windows and gliding doors.

Not only are most exterior sidings composed of wood, but so are most interior surfaces, with the notable exception of dry-wall construction, also called sheet rock or gypsum board. In the vacation home, interior natural-wood surfacing is far more common than painted dry wall.

As for floors, natural wood is the prime choice in almost all vacation-home installations. Wood is also used in most ceiling surfaces. Because vacation homes are often open-beam construction—with the exterior roofing visible *inside* the house, between the supporting beams or purlins—wood is highly popular and frequently used.

Decks, which in the past were called roofless porches or stoops, are an almost universal part of the average vacation home today. The size and location of a deck can make or break the architectural lines of a house.

Why Wood? Since the dawn of time, wood has been one of the most popular building materials used by man. Even though it is not the most permanent construction material, it is easy to shape and fasten, and it lasts long enough to be used extensively for almost all kinds of interior and exterior house work.

Wood is available in a wide range of varieties. It may be hard, soft, smooth, rough, thick, thin, long, short, stiff, or flexible. Because it has great strength and durability, it has always been an extremely useful material.

Types of Wood. There are two kinds of wood—softwood and hardwood. Softwood comes from needle-bearing trees, like pine and fir. Hardwood comes from broad-leaved trees, like oak and ash. "Hard" and "soft" are misnomers; some softwoods are actually harder than hardwoods.

For exterior siding in use on vacation homes, softwoods are usually used: redwood, cedar, Douglas fir, spruce, southern pine, and others.

For interior paneling, hardwoods like maple and oak—and others—are commonly used, although softwood panels are very popular in vacation homes.

Exterior Siding. Although certainly not an exhaustive list by any means, the following should give you some idea of the current most popular exterior sidings in use on vacation and second homes:

Cedar, northern white
Cedar, western red
Cedar, incense
Fir, Douglas
Fir, white
Hemlock
Larch
Pine, lodgepole
Pine, southern
Redwood
Spruce, Sitka
Spruce, Engelmann
Spruce, western white

Many of the above woods are available in log form, in laminated-log form, and in timbers for crib construction.

Shakes and Shingles. Cedar comes not only in board widths for siding but also in the form of shakes and shingles. Both shakes and shingles are thinly sliced rectangles of wood, slightly tapering from bottom to top. A shingle has a smooth surface, a shake is striated.

Shingles and shakes have been popular as siding material since the days of Colonial America. The Cape Cod house is sided in shingles even today. This type of exterior is coming into use once again. As a matter of fact, shakes

and shingles can be used as wall surfaces *inside* today's second home.

Exterior Patterns. The woods mentioned above in board form come in many different types and patterns for use as exterior siding:

Bevel Siding, Horizontal
Board and Batten, Vertical and Horizontal
Board on Board
Bungalow
Colonial
Drop Siding, Horizontal
Shiplap, Horizontal
Tongue and Groove, Vertical and Horizontal
Channel Rustic

Red-cedar shakes used as outside surfacing on this ski cabin in Minnesota. The shakes, which blend in with the mountain site, give an interesting texture to the house's exterior.

Plywood Exterior Siding. Plywood has come to be one of the most important woods in the construction of the vacation home. Not only is plywood used in place of conventional sheathing—that is, the layer of material between stud and outer surface—but it can now be used as sheathing-plus-exterior, *and* as surface for the interior walls of the house.

Plans for plywood homes have already been described in some detail in Chapter Two. In working with plywood you should know something about the various kinds of ply face veneers available, and you should know how to select the kind of ply you want for the specific purpose you have in mind.

Types of Plywood. Plywood is manufactured in two basic types—exterior and interior, with a variety of appearances and quality grades within each type.

Exterior plywood differs from interior only in the kind of glue bond and the grade of veneer used. The adhesive used in exterior plywood has a guaranteed waterproof bond, whereas the adhesive used in interior ply may be either highly moisture-resistant or water proof.

Plywood is made from both hardwoods and softwoods. It is the outer layer of the sheet, called the face veneer, that determines its class.

Softwood plywood face veneer can be redwood, cedar, Douglas fir, hemlock, larch, spruce, knotty pine, white fir, or white pine. The plywood used in cabin and vacation-home construction is usually softwood plywood, except that certain kinds of interior prefinished hardwood plywood panels are used very extensively on inside walls.

Hardwood plywood face veneer can be any of a large number of woods, each of which is usually milled and selected to accentuate the natural beauty of the hardwood grain used.

Every piece of softwood plywood is graded with a letter standardized by the American Plywood Association: N, A, B, C, D, C (plugged), in descending order of quality. Each piece of softwood plywood is also marked either EXT or INT (exterior or interior).

A panel marked A-A has the highest-standard quality veneer on both face and back panels. A-B means there is A appearance on the face panel, B on the back.

A typical exterior paneling in the average vacation home construction would probably be A-C.

Aside from the ordinary plywood, there are various types of special textures and designs available for use as surfaces on vacation homes.

For instance:

APA Texture 1-11 is a type of plywood that has deep grooves cut into the face for sharp shadow lines, simulating individual boards. The grooves are 1/4 inch deep, 3/8 inch wide, 4 inches on center (apart), with the panel thickness 5/8 inch. Texture 1-11 comes with grooves spaced 2 inches on center and 6 and 8 inches on center.

Standard 1-11 has an unsanded face with natural-wood characteristics for rustic effect. It is available with medium-density-overlaid (see below), sanded, rough-sawn (see below), brushed (see below), scratch-sanded, fine-line (see below), or straited (see below) face surfaces. You can finish unsanded and textured surfaces with

Texture 1-11

exterior pigmented stains. It is available in redwood, cedar, Douglas fir, lauan (Philippine mahogany), and southern pine.

Channel Groove has grooves 1/16 inch deep, 3/8 inch wide, cut into faces of 3/8-inch-thick panels, 4 inches on center. It is available in the same finishes and woods as Texture 1-11.

Channel Groove

Reverse Board and Batten features deep, wide grooves cut into brushed, rough-sawn, coarse- or scratch-sanded, or natural-textured surfaces. Grooves are 1/4 inch deep, 1–1½ inches wide, spaced 8, 12, or 16 inches on center, with a panel thickness of 5/8 inch. Deep, sharp shadow lines are featured. It is also available in 3/8- and 1/2-inch-thick panels with 3/32-inch-deep grooves. You can finish it with exterior pigmented stain or leave it natural, without finish, for a weathered, rustic effect. It is available in surfaces and woods the same as Texture 1-11.

Reverse Board and Batten

Fine Line has grooves cut into the face surface to give a distinctive striped effect. The grooving reduces surface checking and gives additional durability to the surface. You can finish it with exterior pigmented stain or exterior acrylic-latex emulsion finish with companion stain-resistant primer. Shallow .08-inch grooves about 1/4 inch on center, 1/32 inch wide. Fine Line comes combined also with Texture 1-11, or channel groove, 2, 4, 8 inches on center, or reverse board and batten.

Fine Line

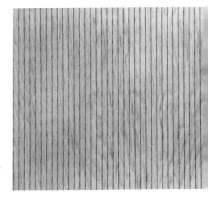

Rough Sawn is a special surface designed to combine the natural look of wood with the ease of installation provided by large panels. It is also available in various types of grooved surfaces.

Kerfed is a light touch-sanded surface, rough sawn with narrow square-cut grooves to provide

Rough Sawn

Kerfed

Brushed

Striated

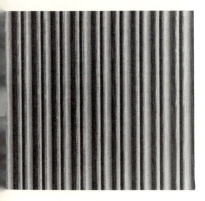
Medium Density Overlaid

a textured effect. The long edges of the panel are shiplapped for a continuous pattern. Grooves are 1/8 inch wide, 1/16 inch deep, and 4 inches on center. It is available also in groove spacings of 2, 6, and 8 inches on-center; also 5/8 inch thick with 1/4-inch-deep grooves for deeper shadow. Available in wood faces the same as Texture 1-11.

Brushed, or relief grain surface, accents the natural-grain pattern to create striking textured surfaces. It is available with Texture 1-11, channel groove, and reverse board and batten groovings—in redwood, Douglas fir, cedar, lauan, Sitka spruce, and white fir.

Striated has fine striations that are random-width, closely spaced grooves forming a vertical pattern. The striations conceal nail heads, joints, checking, and grain raise. You can finish it with exterior latex paint or pigmented stain (see under "Fine Line").

The textured plywood siding above can serve both as a decorative siding *and* as structural sheathing. These textures can also be used—and are particularly effective—in informal settings inside the vacation home, for example, in the family room or even the living room.

PAINT SURFACES

The textured surfaces above can take paint as specified, but if you are looking for *the* perfect plywood paint surface, use medium density overlaid plywood.

Medium Density Overlaid Plywood has a surface that holds paint longer and spreads it faster, cutting down on both labor and paint costs.

MDO comes with V-grooving, providing vertical shadow effect. The grooves are 6 or 8 inches on center. You can finish MDO with exterior house paints with compatible prime and topcoats.

MDO Channel Groove has shallow grooves 1/16 inch deep, 3/8 inch wide, cut into faces of 3/8-inch MDO panels, 4 inches or 2 inches on center. Other groove spacings are available; also, in Texture 1-11 patterns.

MDO Reverse Board and Batten has grooves 1/4 inch deep, 1–1½ inches wide, cut into medium density overlaid surface. Grooves are spaced 12 inches on center, with panels 5/8 inch thick. It features a deep, sharp shadow line. The long edge is shiplapped for a continuous pattern. You can finish the surface as described above.

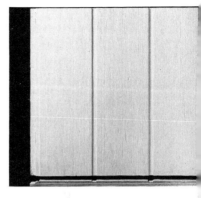

MDO Channel Groove

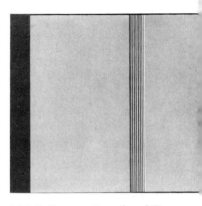

MDO Reverse Board and Batten

HARDBOARD EXTERIOR SIDING

Hardboard paneling comes in various styles for use as exterior siding for the vacation home. This type of reconstituted wood is made of natural-wood fibers that have been compressed into smooth, grainless sheets, either ⅛ inch or ¼ inch thick, and 4 by 8 feet in size.

Hardboard can be worked with ordinary woodworking tools. You fasten the sheets to framing timber with nails, screws, or adhesive. For maximum holding power, use screws.

Siding patterns come in vertical or horizontal positioning, and in many different designs.

Lap siding, a horizontal application, comes in varying widths, usually 6 to 12 inches apart. This style provides strong dramatic shadow lines.

Vertical sidings include V- and U-grooved,

random-grooved, and ungrooved panels. Board and batten applications—with the thin board raised or with the thin board grooved—are also available.

Hardboard sidings are available preprimed or prefinished in wood-grain designs, with rugged hand-sawn appearance, in various colors, smooth surfaced, or with a textured look, such as that of stucco and wood shakes.

ROOFING

A roof can serve as a major architectural element of a house. It can add character to a plain house or detract from an otherwise handsome one. Its design and style can give each individual structure a personality of its own.

There are nine basic roof styles—gable, butterfly, shed, mansard, hip, gambrel, flat, dome, and vault. The first six of these are by far the most popular in vacation homes.

The most prevalent of the six is the *gable*, which is actually an inverted V-shape. Cape Cod cottages and Colonial homes have gable roofs, and so do many other styles, including the ubiq-

Sidings made of hardboard come in several patterns to emulate wooden surfaces. Shown above are smooth-surfaced horizontal lap siding, a new shingle-and-shake design, textured board - and - batten panels, and vertical panels with reverse batten.

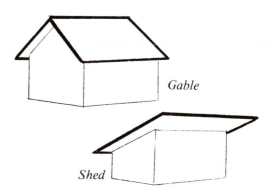

uitous A-frame, which is *all* gable.

The *butterfly* roof is rare, but the *shed* roof, which is one straight sloped plane, is a favorite shape for the beach house and the general vacation home.

The steep slope of the *mansard* is sometimes seen in a second home. The *hip* roof is only rarely used. The *gambrel*—a folded-down gable roof—is Dutch in origin and sometimes is used to give a home a Colonial look.

Roofing Shingles. Although there are many different kinds of roofing materials available for the vacation home, including tarpaper, corrugated sheet metal, and slate, the two most commonly used are wood shingles of cedar and asphalt roofing shingles.

Cedar shakes and shingles have been mentioned earlier in the chapter in reference to exterior siding. The facts are the same for its use as roofing cover.

The most popular type of roofing nowadays is asphalt shingling. This type of construction can give you many different textures and colors, but its most important advantages are its resistance to fire, to wind, and to fungus and algae.

Asphalt shingles are tested and classified by the Underwriters' Laboratories, Inc., for fire resistance, and they bear the UL label.

Hip

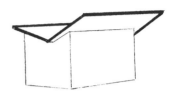
Butterfly

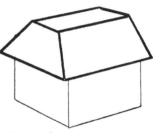
Mansard

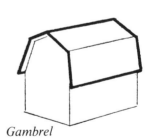
Gambrel

Most asphalt roofing is wind-resistant, fire-resistant, and fungus- and algae-resistant. Self-sealing roof shingles are ideal for installation.

Self-sealing asphalt shingles bear the UL's wind-resistant label. Self-sealers are standard in many parts of the country, and are ideal for any vacation locale.

Fungus- and algae-resistant asphalt shingles are now on the market and are available in a wide variety of textures and colors.

INTERIOR STYLING

An almost endless list of possible interior-paneling surfaces can be used in the vacation home. In addition to the softwoods mentioned under the section "Exterior Styling," there are a number of hardwoods available, too.

The types and patterns of surfacing materials available are almost endless. Random-width vertical paneling is the most popular, but board and batten and board on board are becoming increasingly popular in the informal atmosphere of the typical modern vacation home.

You can always use any type of patterning inside: shiplap, tongue and groove, bevel siding, channel rustic—to name only a few. The sky's the limit these days!

Tips on Using Interior Paneling. Because interior strips of paneling come in varying widths (6, 8, 10, and 12 inches), you can make interesting effects in the wall where it is installed. Soft shadow lines will appear between each piece. Some of these paneling lines will be more distinct than others, depending upon how simple or intricate the edge pattern is.

The shadow lines can be used to do things decoratively in a wide variety of situations. And the wood's grain can be emphasized for a most interesting visual effect.

Here are some ways to apply paneling for special effects:

1. Install paneling vertically to make a low room look higher.
2. Install paneling horizontally to make a short room look longer and lower.
3. Apply paneling so its lines give a directional emphasis, leading the eye to focal points of interest such as a window, a fireplace, or an antique built-in.
4. Install paneling to provide continuity between one room and another: Repeat lines, or use visual emphasis.
5. Create a casual air through the use of "random widths" of paneling.
6. Create a formal air by using only uniform widths of paneling.

Interior Plywood. If you intend to paint the surface of your interior walls, you should finish them off in dry-wall construction. Dry wall gives an excellent paint base, and is in many ways the most satisfactory method for achieving a good painted wall surface.

However, plywood can also be used as a paint base. There are interior types of plywood that take paint very well, both in hardwood and softwood face veneers.

For a good paint finish, use hardwood paneling of sound grade or B-grade. If you want a natural-wood effect, get good or A-grade face in hardwood ply, and then stain it and finish it off as described in Chapter Eleven, "Painting."

Random-width prefinished plywood paneling affords a traditional background for pictures and a restful setting ideal for a vacation house.

Utility-grade ply can be used for backs and concealed areas.

Prefinished Interior Ply. The most commonly used type of interior finishing in the vacation home today is the prefinished plywood panel. There are so many varieties of wood faces available—both hardwood and softwood—that an exhaustive list would be too long to include.

Once you have attached prefinished plywood paneling to the wall studs, your wall-surface maintenance days are over. All that is necessary is to clean and polish the surface infrequently.

Interior Hardboard. Prefinished hardboard panels are also available for interior wall surfaces. These hardboard sheets can be applied exactly like prefinished plywood paneling and give years of minimal-maintenance service.

There is a wide range of wood grains, colors, and many different patterns and textures.

Hardboard is extremely durable material and takes hard abuse without denting, marring, or scuffing. It is virtually children-proof. All the maintenance needed is an occasional wiping with a damp cloth.

FLOORING SURFACES

Most vacation-home floors are finished in wood. Some are simply thick plywood used as combined underlayment and final floor.

Any wood floor can be stained or simply clear-varnished. (See Chapter Eleven.)

Vinyl tile can be applied directly to underlayment plywood for a finish surface. This type of tile can stand up under a real beating and is quite good for the surface of the vacation home that gets most of the traffic.

You can use indoor-outdoor carpeting in more informal installations. Carpeting and resilient floor tiles are discussed more fully in Chapter Twelve.

Wood Floors. The most popular type of wooden floors are simple oak planks in tongue-and-groove stripping. These strips come in all different color tones and sizes. A most unusual and interesting effect is that obtained by the use of Old English Plank—an imitation of random-width planks, prefinished to a deep dark color and then secured to the floor by wooden pegs or wrought-head antique ship's nails.

Old English Plank (left) is a random-width plank floor, fastened to the joists by wrought-head antique ship's nails. Ranch Plank (right) an adaptation of Old English flooring, comes in random widths with wooden pegs for fasteners.

Ranch Plank is an adaptation of Old English flooring. It comes in random widths, too, with pegs inserted in the prefinished planking.

Wood floors also can be laid in pecan, or in cedar, and in a variety of other woods, both hardwood and softwood, including beech, maple, and birch. Hardwood floors stand up under usage better than softwood floors; however, there is a great deal of warmth and color in softwoods like cedar.

Another design of wooden flooring quite popular in the more informal second home is the parquet floor—a floor made of wooden squares, like a giant chessboard. In olden days, it might be noted, before the use of modern tile floors, parquet floors were the most elegant and expensive kind of wooden floor obtainable.

Parquet floor tiles come in various sizes and in a wide variety of colors and prefinished tones. Generally they are oak or pecan.

Tile Floors. There are two kinds of tile floors—ceramic tile and resilient tile.

Resilient tile is the tile found most often in houses today. It is durable to wear and tear, and it is easy to maintain. You can usually get away with simply cleaning and waxing it, rather than refinishing it and then waxing it as you might a wooden floor.

Resilient tiles come in a variety of shapes, sizes, and designs. Many of them are manufactured to simulate conventional ceramic tiles both in squares and in terrazzo combinations. These patterns imitate brick floors, wooden floors, designs copied from Mediterranean villas, from churches, and from other European and Eastern sources. The varieties are endless—and they add a great deal of color and brightness to the floor.

Such designs can be used to great advantage in the informal setting of a second home.

Ceramic Tiles. True ceramic tiles are the best tiles to use for any floor, of course. A ceramic tile lasts longer, and—after all—it *is* the real thing. But ceramic costs more and because of the difficulty in laying it and the expense of masonry help, ceramic is not quite so popular as it once was with the person on a limited budget.

Resilient-tile floors come in many designs, one of which is simulated brick —a cushioned vinyl surface that takes rugged treatment and provides an authentic Colonial look.

CEILING

The vacation home frequently has a very simple type of ceiling: it is composed of wooden roof planks showing through behind the roof beams or purlins.

However, many times this is a false illusion; the planking you see may be plywood veneer, with the actual roof a layer above that, possibly separated by a layer of insulation.

Some ceilings are made of soundproof insulated tile, but more and more the average vacation home sports wood of one kind or another in its walls, floors, and ceilings.

Textured - oak - grain planks in this A-Frame ceiling are actually a plastic-finished hardboard material that can be applied easily over ceiling joists.

Chapter 11

PAINTING

BECAUSE so many vacation homes these days are erected as shells, finishing up has become a top-priority feature with scores of new home owners.

Finishing up includes many things, but its least complicated and most important phase is painting. All wood surfaces, and the surfaces of most other materials as well, need painting, both inside and outside the house.

Since more than eight out of ten vacation homes are of wood-frame construction, it is necessary to know not only how to put on an original paint finish, but also how to maintain it later on. All wood houses need to be painted mainly to preserve the wood, but also to add color and beauty to the exterior.

Frequently, the basic charm of a wood-frame house is the distinctive look of the wood grain.

An outstanding pattern should be covered with clear preservative to protect the grain against the elements, or possibly with a stain to enhance the color of the wood, and with a varnish over that.

EXTERIOR PAINT

Several types of paint are used for vacation-house exteriors. A good outdoor paint should be little affected by moisture. It should be resistant to staining by rust and other residues from metal corrosion. And it should resist mildew.

No one type of paint has all these desirable characteristics, but you can depend on today's high-quality paints to perform well under most of these conditions.

Try to find out from your local paint dealer what types of house paint are best for your local conditions.

House Paints. A house paint consists of two parts: of solids, or pigments, and of liquids, or vehicles. The pigment hides, colors, and extends the color. The vehicle consists of a drying oil, a thinner, like mineral spirits or turpentine, and a small amount of paint dryer.

Two basic types of paint are commonly used on vacation-house exteriors: oil-base paints and water-base paints.

An oil-base paint is one that uses linseed oil as its vehicle and lead as its pigment. There are titanium-lead-zinc formulations, too. Linseed oil makes the paint film soft and flexible and highly resistant to cracking and flaking. The main objections to oil paint are its low hiding power,

its off-white color, and its tendency to retain dirt.

There are also multiple-pigment oil paints, with varying contents of titanium, lead, and zinc pigments. These paints give brilliant color that remains uniformly clean in service. They are durable and wear away slowly. On the other hand, multiple-pigment paints are hard to maintain, and they do not present a good repaint surface.

A water-base paint is also called a latex paint. The most common kind of latex is emulsion paint, with the major types polyvinyl-acetate (PVA) paint and acrylic paint. These water-base paints are permeable to moisture and less likely to blister than oil paints. A latex dries quickly to a flat sheen; it is easy to apply and clean.

Latex has good color retention. Frequently a latex paint requires an oil-base primer; it simply does not bond well to wood. The oil-base primer

Medium Density Plywood is especially recommended for use as a good paint base. The solid panels in this house give brightness and bounce to the design.

minimizes grain raise due to the water in the latex paint. Latex spreads thinner than oil; it is always recommended to use two coats of latex in addition to the primer in exterior applications.

Alkyd resin paint is a paint with a synthetic resin used as a modifying agent and vehicle. An alkyd paint is easy to apply, is quick-drying, and has good color retention. It produces flat or semigloss sheens. In some cases, a primer is unnecessary.

Painting the Vacation House. The most common paints to use for second homes are the brighter and deeper colors, rather than self-cleaning whites, which are the mainstay of non-leisure-home applications. If you do use a white paint, select the nonchalking type, especially if the surface below the paint can be stained by chalking.

If mildew is a threat in the vacation site where you settle, you can obtain mildew-resistant paints or have mildewcide added to your primer and finish coats.

When the paint film becomes noticeably thin after a season or two, you should repaint the surface. If the coating has peeled, remove all the loose paint with a wire brush. Then carefully brush a primer into all checks and on all exposed wood surfaces. The top coats can be applied after the primer has dried.

Stains. The easiest of finishes to apply is a stain, although, once applied, it must be renewed more frequently than paint. Since many vacation homes feature wood grain as a siding, the use of stain is widespread to accentuate the pattern.

A *penetrating stain* colors the wood, tones down the grain, but leaves little or no surface film.

An *opaque stain* has more pigment, produces a uniform color that almost hides the grain, dries flat, and leaves a thin surface coating.

With all stains, you can expect some checking and surface roughening. This merely enhances the general appearance of unsanded or textured surfaces.

Apply stain to a clean, dry surface only, in one or more coats, as recommended by the manufacturer. Renew the stain when weathering or fading occurs.

Painting Plywood. When you are dealing with plywood outer surfaces, you may either paint or stain, depending partially upon the type of plywood surface you use. Some types of unsanded rustic-type panels, and the popular Texture 1-11, are designed to be finished with a highly pigmented opaque stain. As for regular sanded A-C or B-C grade panels, you can either stain them or use them as a low-cost base for paint.

Medium Density Overlaid Plywood is a type of panel manufactured specifically for use in vacation houses that demand a good paint base. Standard grades of plywood will check or crack under a paint finish. MDO Plywood resists checking and grain raise and will add life to any paint finish.

However, MDO panels will *not* accept a stain finish. Make up your mind between paint and stain before you select the type of exterior material used.

When painting plywood, it is important to

apply the prime coat and seal the edges as soon as possible. Edges of plywood absorb moisture rapidly and should be coated thoroughly with a top-quality primer, preferably before they arrive at the building site.

The primer coat is the key to all good painting and should be applied as soon as plywood panels are in place—before, if possible. If you intend to use a deep-colored top coat, you can tint the primer to reduce the contrast between primer and top coat.

Shingles and Shakes. Shingles and shakes are extremely popular as siding material for second homes. Most of these are made from Western red cedar, a free-splitting wood that combines a pleasing color and attractive grain with a remarkable resistance to decay.

Several types of coating can be used to finish them, essentially distinguished by the amount of pigment contained in each.

Stain. A quality stain is made with a penetrating-type oil and usually provides a flat finish in either a semitransparent or solid color. Where natural wood grain and texture are desired in an exterior, shingle stains are unexcelled. They are available in several wood tones. It is possible with stain to maintain the beautiful natural look of cedar better than with clear treatments. Always follow directions; proper mixing and application are essential.

Paint. Exterior latex paint is probably the best kind to use if you wish to *cover* a shingle or shake surface. This type of paint deposits a film that is more porous than high-gloss oil paint and is more likely to allow the escape of moisture

This house, called the Mushroom House, in Bolinas, California, is faced with red cedar shingles sixteen inches long.

without blistering, cracking, or peeling.

Wood Preservative. To preserve a natural grain, coat the shingle or shake with a clear wood preservative. Pentachlorophenol, creosote, phenyl-mercury-oleate, and various metallic salts, such as copper neaphthenate, are used as water-resistant wood preservatives and are usually effective in resisting rot and decay and in discouraging the growth of molds and other vegetation on the surface of cedar shingles and shakes.

Bleach. A natural gray appearance can be obtained by using a weathering and bleaching compound on shingles or shakes. These solutions speed up the natural weathering process.

Varnish. Varnish or lacquer has not proved successful in preserving the natural color and grain of shingles.

Trim Paint. For all exterior trim—wood, screen frames, shutters—use specially made exterior trim paints. Some of the qualities to look for in a good trim enamel are good color, one-coat hiding, good leveling, gloss retention, rapid drying, freedom from brush marks, high gloss, and good durability.

Exterior enamel, which dries with a relatively glossy surface, is available in either water- or oil-base mixtures and in a variety of sheens, from high-gloss for very smooth surfaces to semigloss for those not so smooth.

Masonry Surfaces. Clear coatings of paint help brick, cement, stucco, cinder block, and asbestos cement withstand the weather and also allow the natural appearance of the material to show through.

Use a cement-base paint on a masonry surface, or a more colorful rubber-base coating in a vinyl-and-alkyd emulsion paint. If the surface preparations are done properly, any exterior house paint can be used on masonry.

Asphalt shingles used as siding require a special treatment calling for exterior emulsions formulated specifically for this surface.

Metallic Surfaces. Galvanized iron, tin, and steel building materials must also be painted to avoid rusting. If copper is not painted, it will give off a corrosive wash, and aluminum will corrode.

Use regular house paint or exterior enamel on any metallic surface, or get a special rust-inhibitive coating if the situation requires it.

How Much Paint to Use. A finish coat of house paint is usually applied at a rate of 500 square feet of surface per gallon. Primer will cover about 450 square feet per gallon.

Here is a simple rule of thumb for estimating the amount of paint needed to finish the exterior surface of a house:

1. Find out the height of the house (in feet), measuring the distance from the foundation to the eaves for a flat house; for a pitched-roof house, add 2 feet.

2. Measure the distance around the foundation (in feet) to obtain the second figure. Multiply that figure by the average height to obtain the surface area in square feet.

3. Divide the surface area by 450 to find the number of gallons of primer required.

4. Divide the surface area by 500 to find the number of gallons of finish paint required for each coat.

INTERIOR SURFACES

Interior paints also come in oil-base and water-base formulations.

Use an *oil-base paint* where there is a definite need for washability, durability, and a flat appearance. Fingerprints, dirt, and crayon can be repeatedly scrubbed off from an oil-base surface. Use alkyd-resin-base enamels for trim; they have good hiding properties. Alkyd resins can be brushed, rolled, or sprayed on. Some of them are self-priming on wood.

A water-base paint is an emulsion of resin-polyvinyl acetate, acrylic, or styrene-butadiene latex mixed with water. It can be washed, but not scrubbed. Usually called a *latex paint*, it can be applied with brush, roller, or spray.

Latex Finishes. Latex is the do-it-yourselfer's dream paint. It is easy to apply, and it gives

Special texture paints must be applied in ways recommended by the manufacturers, as illustrated here.

instant professional results. A latex paint is quick-drying and so makes it possible for you to complete the job fast. In addition, cleaning up is very simple: a combination of soap and water is all that is needed.

Water-thinned paint is made from many different materials, depending on the type of binder, or vehicle, used. It is sometimes referred to as vinyl, PVA, or acrylic. Most of the new latexes are emulsions of polymers or copolymers in water, with suitable pigments, stabilizers, and preservatives added.

Latex works very simply. After the paint has been applied, the emulsion coalesces and permits the water to evaporate, leaving the paint film of pigment and vehicle on the surface.

Do not use latex directly over iron or steel surfaces. Use a rust-inhibitive primer first, then apply latex.

Latex paint spreads readily and can be applied by brush, roller, or spray. There is only one precaution you should take: Because the paint goes on so easily, do not allow it to spread too thinly, or you will diminish the cover power.

Water-base paint dries in an amazingly short time—from half an hour to one and a half hours. But its quick-drying properties may create problems on an exterior surface. The paint may dry too quickly, causing lap and brush marks to show. On interior surfaces, no such problem arises.

Unlike an oil-base paint, latex can be applied on a humid or dampish day without affecting the drying properties of the paint film. Latex allows moisture trapped inside the walls to escape, minimizing peeling or blistering. Do not apply latex to a soaking-wet surface, however.

A good-quality latex paint gives clean, bright colors and offers good durability. Any dirt or grime that appears on the surface can be washed off with a mild detergent and water.

Natural Finish. The natural finish of woodwork in a vacation home is of course the most popular type of interior surfacing used today. If you have installed paneling of any kind that is not prefinished, you can always stain it lightly to bring out the color and grain, or you can paint it for solid-color blocks.

Stain. To stain, first apply a coat of sealer to cut down the grain contrast of the wood. Some manufacturers make companion stains and sealers that can be mixed to stain *and* seal in one coat.

Oil stain of all kinds is available. Brush or wipe the stain on, then wipe it to the proper depth, or color, that you want.

Finish. To add luster and durability to any interior-surface wood, apply a clear finish, such as high-quality nitrocellulose, lacquer, or a good varnish. You can use a satin finish, a flat finish, or semigloss or gloss, depending on your personal preference. Then add two coats of a clear finish to achieve a uniform gloss.

Special Natural Finishes. If you are interested in bringing out the grain in either paneling or plywood, select these wood patterns carefully for their appearance, and then use one of the special natural finishes that have been developed for this purpose.

Color toning requires companion stains and nonpenetrating sealers. You can apply stain and sealer in one step. Tint a small amount of sealer with stain until you get the desired tone. Test it on a sample piece of wood. Mix enough stain and sealer to do the entire job and apply it with brush or spray. Dry, sand lightly, and apply a clear finish to give the desired luster and durability. The sealer preserves the natural wood appearance. You can use tones of light gray, brown, or tan—all of these go well with wood colors and provide excellent grain masking.

Light stain is an alternate method of applying a natural finish that mellows the grain pattern of wood. It requires more steps than color toning, but it does not require companion stains and sealers. Whiten the panel with pigmented resin sealer or interior white undercoat cut 1 to 1 with thinner. Before it becomes tacky, wipe the sealer off to let the grain show through. Apply clear resin sealer, allow it to dry, and sandpaper it lightly. Add color with tinted undercoat, thin enamel, pigmented resin sealer, or light stain, apply it thinly, and wipe it down to the proper color depth. Dry it. Sand it lightly. Apply a coat of satin varnish or brushing lacquer to provide luster and durability.

Stippled. For stippled effect, prime the wood with an oil-base primer. Then apply stipple finish.

Multicolor spatter finish. Use a lacquer, blending two or more colors of uniform fleck size. Apply them with spray equipment; the colors will remain separate and distinct, creating an unusual effect. Lacquer for this type of finish is available in aerosol spray cans. Apply the finish coat lightly over the colored background, or with full flecks over a primer. You can work out any number of interesting effects with this method of spattering.

Interior Trim. For interior trim, you can use oil-base or water-base paints. Interior latex semigloss enamels have the very same good qualities that all other latex paints have. They cover well, are durable, and the cleaning up after the job is very simple.

Hardwood-Floor Finish. The most commonly used wood for flooring, as has been mentioned, is oak, although hard maple is also used, along with cedar, beech, birch, and pecan. The kind of wood has no influence on the applied finish except in special cases.

The first step in finishing a floor is the process of staining.

Stain is used on floors for the same reasons it is used on exterior and interior paneling—to bring out the color of the wood and accentuate the grain. After applying stain with a rag and wiping it until the desired color tone has been attained, you should let it dry overnight before the next finishing operation.

If the color of the wood is satisfactory as it is, you can always omit the stain.

If you are staining softwoods like pine, gum, cedar, or redwood, apply a "wash coat" of shellac before staining to help ensure uniform porosity for uniform staining. With other woods you do not need a wash coat.

Filling. Hardwood, especially oak, has pores that show small depressions in the wood. Use a floor filler to fill these pores. Apply it with a brush and then wipe off the excess with burlap.

Each panel in this interior has been painted a different color to break up the wall space into bright solid patterns.

Fillers are available in almost any color needed to match the wood.

Sealer. A floor sealer is a penetrating coat that is used as a protective finish for hardwood flooring. The sealer penetrates the fibers of the wood to form a wear-resistant surface that does not extend above the level of the wood and prevents additional coats of paint from seeping in.

Apply sealer in liberal coatings. After it has dried, buff the surface with steel wool.

Varnish. One of the best finishes for a floor is varnish, available in several degrees of gloss—high, medium, and low. A high-gloss varnish is more wear-resistant than a low-gloss one.

A varnish needs adequate time to dry—at least overnight; twenty-four hours is better. If a sealer is not used, at least two coats of varnish must be applied to obtain a uniform appearance.

Follow directions carefully in applying varnish. Each manufacturer uses a different formulation.

Clear. If the floor of your vacation home will get a lot of traffic, you can use one of the new urethane finishes. Urethane comes in three types: urethane oil, which looks and acts like a conventional varnish; moisture-cured urethane, which dries by reaction with moisture in

the air; or two-component urethane, which must be mixed just before use and which has limited pot life after mixing.

Read and follow carefully the directions of the manufacturer.

Shellac. This light-colored, fast-drying floor finish is easy to apply with a clean wide brush. Allow the first coat to dry for two to four hours. Then sand it lightly for a smooth finish.

The second coat should be hard enough to walk on after another four hours. Where there is heavy traffic, use three coats.

Wax. Waxing protects the finish of any floor. It should not be applied to unfinished wood because it penetrates the wood and is hard to remove. Wax itself is not a durable finish, but it will protect the real finish as long as it is intact.

Use two coats of wax on a newly finished floor. If you apply liquid wax, use several coats in order to build up the film. Liquid wax, incidentally, is thinner than paste wax to begin with.

Always seal new wood before waxing to prevent dirt from penetrating the wood grain. A coat of three-pound cut of shellac is an excellent wood sealer.

Waxing increases the wear resistance and water repellency of shellac. Let a shellac finish dry for twenty-four to forty-eight hours before waxing. Paste wax is recommended for use on shellacked floors.

Painting Floors. Although homeowners usually seek to preserve the wood grain in floors when finishing a hardwood surface, there is growing interest in floors finished with colored enamels. The idea is to color the floor to match walls or draperies or to blend it in with the furniture coverings. This is particularly true of the more informal interiors in leisure homes.

Floor enamels come in such a wide variety of colors that there is no limit to the number of pleasing decorative schemes it is possible to achieve.

Floor and deck enamels can be used to restore original flooring in older vacation homes. A pigmented urethane material can be used on a floor where abrasion resistance is required. The pigment will not affect the properties of the urethane paint.

Sanding and filling must be done carefully to prepare the flooring for painting. When the filler is dry, use three coats of self-sealing floor enamel. Let each coat dry thoroughly before adding the next. Then put on a coat of wax to help protect the enamel and to give additional luster to the floor.

REPAINTING EXTERIOR SURFACES

Assuming that a first coat of exterior paint is of 4½–5 mils thickness (.0045 to .005 inch), it will take three to five years to wear away enough white or light-colored mixed pigment paint to require one new coat of paint, or six years to require two new coats.

White lead and oil paint wears away half again as fast as mixed-pigment paint. Dark-colored paint wears away more slowly than light-colored paint. A dark-colored surface needs to be repainted about every six years only.

Various paints wear differently. Some develop fine checks that slowly deepen and multiply, causing the paint to crumble away. Other paints wear by erosion.

Water is the primary cause of paint decay. Rain seeps in *behind* siding or soffits or other painted surfaces, and the moisture passes out *through* the paint, causing cracking and blistering.

Poor-quality paint or a skimpy two-coat job can cause excessively fast degeneration. Incompatible paints sometimes cause one coat to flake or peel from the other.

A stain does not normally crack, curl, flake, or blister. If stain needs to be refinished, it is usually done to add life to faded colors or to restain bare wood spots.

Repainting Procedure. You should repaint before a coat of paint is in such bad shape that extensive refinishing operations are required. Then follow these steps:

1. With a wire brush, remove all loose paint. Sand the old coat to remove surface roughness.

2. Prime the area with a top-quality exterior house paint primer. Either an original or a repaint coating is more durable when applied over an adequate house-paint primer.

3. Apply one coat of the house paint produced by the primer manufacturer. Use two top coats if the original coating shows excessive wear.

USING A PAINTING CONTRACTOR

If you have enough money and do not want the responsibility of doing the painting yourself, you can always hire a painting contractor to do the job for you.

Dealing with a painting contractor is similar to dealing with a building contractor or an architect, as discussed in Chapter Eight.

First be sure the painting contractor is a reputable man, and then get a signed proposal, estimate, or contract before going ahead.

There are three different quality ranges in the type of job a reputable paint contractor will offer:

Premium. This is a job that will give the best finish possible and provide the maximum durability that can be expected from a painted surface.

Standard. This is a job that has the usual life expectancy of a well-painted surface anywhere.

Minimum. This is a job that, as the term implies, will provide a minimum of durability and appearance benefits to improve the present surface conditions.

Proposal, Estimate, or Contract. The following points should be included in an estimate, proposal, or contract:

1. A specific price for the job.

2. A statement of the number of coats of paint to be applied to each surface, plus spot-priming, if required.

3. A statement showing when the job will be completed, with allowance made for unpredictable weather.

4. A listing of the types and brands of paints to be used.

5. A listing of each area in your home that is to be painted.

6. A statement that the contractor will use drop cloths and other measures to protect your premises, both indoors and outdoors.

7. A statement that the contractor will also remove all leftover materials, leaving your home safe and clean.

Chapter 12

BUILT-INS

THERE are many kind of built-in pieces of furniture that you can add to your second home: banquettes or low couches fastened to the wall and covered with foam-rubber cushions; breakfast tables that fold down from the wall; bunk beds in a sleeping loft; cupboards for the storage of everything from clothing to kitchenware; room dividers; bookcases along the walls; chests of drawers in the bedroom; shelving for closets, cupboards, and cabinets; drawers for recessed storage areas; and almost anything else you can think of.

DOORS

A door for a storage space or step-in closet is not really a "built-in," but it can be constructed in a very simple way.

Assemble the pieces to be put together flat

Typical vacation home shows draperies at a minimum, wall hangings simple, furniture small and utilitarian, and all pieces scaled low and comfortable.

on the floor as illustrated in the accompanying picture, with the tongues fitting snugly into the grooves if you are using tongue and groove, or with the strips fitted tightly together if you are using untongued wood.

Lay a piece of 1-by-2-inch stripping cut two inches narrower than the final width of the door, and center it on the paneling for the door. Tack the crosspiece onto the paneling. Repeat the same procedure near the opposite end.

Place a 1-by-2-inch strip diagonally across the two pieces already in place, mark, and cut at the angle. Lay the diagonal piece in place and tack.

Use wood screws to hold the pieces in place permanently. When the door is finished, use a hand plane to trim off the exposed tongue and groove.

ROOM DIVIDER

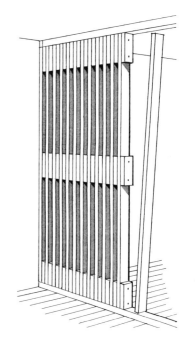

A slat room divider is the simplest kind of spacemaker to build, as illustrated here.

First, nail a 2-by-4 to the floor and to the ceiling so that they are in direct vertical alignment with each other. Be sure that you have nailed each into joists, rather than simply into space beyond the floor or ceiling.

Using 1-by-4 strips of lumber, nail the first piece into the wall.

Now nail the blocking pieces—whatever size you want—into the first piece nailed to the wall.

Then nail a long piece and alternately assemble the divider until you have filled the needed area.

You can toenail in the last piece of lumber to hold it in place. Using a nail set, punch the nail out of sight and cover the hole with wood putty.

DRAWERS

The illustration here shows exactly how to build a drawer. You should first of all find the exact size—height, depth, and width—that you want. Then mark the pieces of wood.

A dado is a groove cut into the wood. The dado at the bottom of the front piece on the drawer illustrated should not be more than one fourth of the thickness of the piece of wood. The same goes for the dadoes where sides join front and back pieces.

Use glue *and* nails in dado joints.

You can use any kind of sheet material for the drawer bottom.

Every drawer built needs some kind of frame-

work to hold it. A typical drawer framework is made out of 1-by-2-inch strips, or smaller ones, if required. The illustration shows a typical installation.

It is important that the sides are square for easy movement of drawers. You can see that this framework is designed for drawers to fit flush with the guides.

Let the back strip of the framework extend about a quarter inch above the side guides to serve as a stop.

This drawer framework can be attached to the back of a closet, or simply against a wall. Or it can serve as an independent unit, which can be moved to any portion of the room or house.

SHELVING

Built-in shelving is one of the easiest of all built-ins to construct.

The simplest construction is shown at the left. The uprights and shelves are made of material of the same width—eight, ten, or twelve inches wide. The cleats, or support pieces, are made of 1-by-2 stripping.

To prevent sagging do not let the shelves exceed twenty-four inches in length without full-width bracing.

A more complicated type of shelving construction is shown at the left. The grooves in the uprights are called dadoes. The dado should be exactly the thickness of the shelf material to allow the shelving to fit into the notch for a perfect appearance.

Bookshelves are usually eight inches deep and nine inches high for average-size books, or twelve inches deep and twelve inches high for larger volumes.

If you want movable shelving, you can buy hardware for making adjustable bookshelves.

CLOSETS

A closet is a most important built-in in a leisure home. Storage space is always in short supply. The best closet is one built in with the house itself. However, if you need more closet space, you can always build your own and attach it to the corner of the room.

The plan shows you how to construct a good, solid closet.

Use 1-by-4-inch strips to start and nail them to the floor. Attach similar strips to the ceiling or joists.

For studs, use 2-by-4 timber, toenailed at the bottom and top to the 1-by-4 strips. Set them sixteen inches apart, on centers, and brace them with 2-by-4-inch fire stops.

Install a prehung door in the door frame for the best result.

Cover the outside of the closet partitions with paneling and the inside with cedar, nailing the paneling and cedar to the fire stops, the top and bottom strips, and the sill.

The minimum inside width of the closet should be twenty-five inches. The length of the closet depends on how much available space is needed.

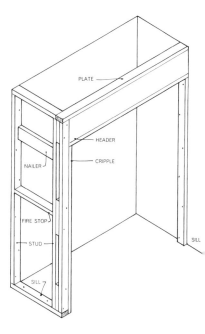

Chapter 13

HEATING

Every vacation home needs some kind of heating device, even if it is only a small wood stove or an electric radiant heater. The more elaborate the house is, the more complicated the heating system must be.

Before considering the kind of heat you may want to install in your second home, you must consider the quality of insulation in the house. Its efficiency will have a lot to do with the kind of heating you eventually choose.

INSULATION

A poorly insulated house will cost you more to heat, not only because of the more expensive heating system necessary, but also because of the larger amount of fuel you will use. It is essential to tighten up as much as possible on the insulation properties of your second home if you wish to save on your heating system and fuel.

Insulating the house may be a part of your "finishing off" program if you have purchased a structure completed only to the shell stage. It is easy to insulate, and the job can be done without a great deal of skill or knowledge.

The places to insulate are an unfinished attic space, under the floor of an unheated crawl space, and all outside walls. Ceilings and the outside walls of any additional rooms added onto a structure must be insulated too.

Home insulating materials fall into one of four categories: loose fill, reflective foil, rigid panel, and flexible blanket, or batt.

Loose fill, consisting of granular or fibrous material, such as mineral wool or vermiculite, comes in large bags and can be poured over attic crawl-space floors between the rafters.

Reflective insulation, usually aluminum foil with one or more layers with air spaces in between, can be applied flush against the wall paneling or in contact with the wall sheathing.

Rigid panels are insulation sheets applied to the inside of walls and ceiling. Some can be used as finished paneling.

Flexible insulation in *blanket,* or *batt,* form is the most commonly used type of insulation available to the homeowner. It comes in 4-to-8-foot lengths, in varying thicknesses from 1 to 6 inches, and in 16-inch widths to fit between standard 16-inch on-center studs. The batt is faced with a paper front and back, with paper flanges running down both sides, by means of which the batt is nailed or stapled to the studs.

Mineral wool, fiber glass, or wood fiber is used inside the batt to serve as insulating material.

All walls as well as the roof and floor should be insulated. Generally speaking, the roof of a house is the part most vulnerable to heat escape and should therefore be the best insulated.

HEATING SYSTEMS

A number of heating systems are available for the vacation home, roughly divided into three basic types: warm-air heat, hot-water and steam heat, and electric heat.

Hot-Air Heat. The simplest heating device of all is the ordinary stove, a typical example of which is the Franklin stove. It is the basic type of hot-air heater.

Stove. The simple stove is cheaper to operate than a central heating system, which is the most complex type of warm-air heater, but a stove is dirtier, requires more attention, and disseminates heat less uniformly than the central system.

A wood-burning or coal-burning stove heats the air by radiation. A stove can be used to provide heat for a circulated air system, in which case the stove is attached to a network of ducts that send the heat into all the rooms.

Four fuels are commonly used to provide heat in a warm-air system: wood, coal, oil, or gas. The properties, both advantages and disadvantages, of these four types of fuel are discussed later on in this chapter.

Circulator heater. A circulator heater is a simple stove with some kind of air circulator attached; a fan or blower is usually used. This

type of heater can effectively heat four or five small rooms, but it cannot be depended on to give uniform heat. The distance from the heater to the center of each room to be heated should not be more than eighteen feet.

Pipeless furnace. In a small vacation home, a "pipeless" furnace may be used with some success. Such a furnace, located under the floor, discharges warm air through a single register usually placed directly above the furnace. Units that burn wood, coal, gas, or oil are available for second homes designed with crawl spaces or basements. Gas- and oil-burning units, for suspension beneath a floor, are available for vacation homes without basements.

Gas-fired heater. A small gas-fired heater is another type of warm-air heater in use. It can be recessed in the walls of any room of the house.

The wood stove requires a great deal of attention, and does not spread the heat uniformly through the room, but in a moderate climate it is perfectly adequate.

Such a unit can be controlled manually or by thermostat. The burning gas heats the air, which circulates around the room. Heater vents carry off the burned gases.

Forced-warm-air heater. When a stove or simple heating unit is unable to provide enough heat to warm a vacation home, a more complex system—a forced-warm-air type—can be installed. Such a system consists of a furnace, ducts, and registers. A blower in the furnace pushes the warm air to the rooms through supply ducts and registers. Return grilles and ducts carry back the cooled air, which is reheated and then recirculated.

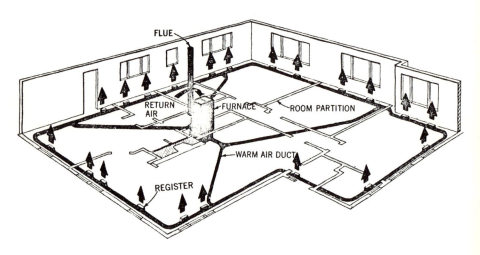

The perimeter-loop heating system is one of the most successful types of forced-warm-air heating systems in use in the vacation home.

Combined heater and cooler. The beauty of the forced-warm-air system is its versatility. By the addition of cooling coils, it can be adapted into a forced-cool-air system to cool the house in the summertime. A combination heating-and-cooling system may be installed; this provides the most efficient and best-controlled environment possible in a second home.

Humidifier. A humidifier can be installed to add moisture to the house air and avoid the discomfort and other disadvantages of a too-dry atmosphere in cold weather.

Ducts and Grilles. Duct outlets that supply the heat to each room in a forced-warm-air system should be located along outside walls of the house—low in the wall, in the baseboard, or in the floor, where they do not blow air directly on occupants of the room.

A typical installation has a cold-air return located in each room. When supply outlets are located on outside walls, the return grilles should be located along the inside walls—in the baseboard or in the floor. When the supply outlets are along inside walls, the return grilles should be along outside walls.

Return grilles that are centrally located work fine with what is called a perimeter-type forced-warm-air heating system. One return may be enough for a relatively small second home. The perimeter-loop-type of heating system is the most common type of forced-warm air system used in the typical vacation home. All the outlets are along outside walls, with the return grille in the center of the house. This type of system was originally designed for concrete-slab construction. A perimeter-loop system can work efficiently only in a tightly insulated house.

Hot Water and Steam Heat. A hot-water or steam-heat system consists of a boiler, pipes, and room heating units, which can be either radiators or convectors. The hot water or steam is circulated through pipes to the radiators or convectors. From there, the heat flows into the room.

Boilers for hot-water or steam-heat systems are designed for burning coal, gas, or oil.

In a hot-water or steam system, an ordinary radiator is set on the floor or mounted on the wall of the room to be heated, with newer types of radiators designed to be recessed into the wall to provide more room and avoid unsightly shapes. A radiator may be partially or fully enclosed in a cabinet. Openings at the top and bottom provide air circulation. The best place for a radiator is under a window.

Baseboard radiator. A baseboard radiator is a hollow or finned unit designed to simulate a conventional wood baseboard. It can heat a well-insulated room uniformly.

Convector. A convector has finned tubes enclosed in a cabinet with openings at the top and bottom. Hot water or steam circulates through the tubes, warming the air and pushing it out at the top.

A forced-hot-water system is usually intended for a large house, and while it is not quite suited to a small vacation home, it can be used in a larger one. A circulator pushes the water through the entire system, which works from a gas- or oil-fired boiler.

A steam heating system is somewhat old-fashioned now and has largely been replaced by forced-hot-water or warm-air systems. There is too much heat lag in the steam heating system for modern usage.

Forced-hot-water or steam systems can also be used in connection with radiant-panel heating. The water or steam circulates through pipes hidden in the walls and is transmitted to the rooms through radiation and convection as the walls, floor, or ceiling—wherever the pipes are located—are warmed. The wall, floor, or ceiling itself acts as the "radiator."

Actually, the hot-water and steam systems are too cumbersome and complicated for the average second home. However, some large leisure homes used for year-round occupancy will find these systems practicable and, in fact, the only efficient ones to use.

Electric Heat. There are many different types and designs of electric heating equipment available for the vacation home. The most common ones are: ceiling unit, baseboard heat, heat pump, central furnace, floor furnace, and wall unit.

Most electric-powered units are resistance-type heaters, producing heat when a high-resistance element heats as electric current passes through it, the same way an electric radiant heater works.

Ceiling heat can be provided with an electric heating cable laid behind the surface of the ceiling.

Baseboard-heat units resemble ordinary wood baseboards, with the heating element hidden from view. The unit is sometimes used under a large picture window in conjunction with ceiling heat.

Heat pump. The heat pump can heat and cool. In winter, it takes heat from the outdoor air to warm a house or room. In summer it removes heat from the house or room and discharges it into the outside air.

Central furnace. The most complicated system of electric heating available is a development of the forced-warm-air system. The electric-powered forced-air central heating system requires ducts similar to those described under forced-air central-heating systems. Wall units, either radiant- or convection-type, can be recessed or installed on any wall surface. These units contain various types of resistance-heating elements. The warm air may be circulated by gravity or by means of an electric fan.

Each room heated by this type of equipment usually has a thermostat to hold the air in it to a desired temperature.

BURNERS AND FUELS

Four fuels are commonly used for home heating: wood, coal, oil, and gas.

Electricity is not a fuel but a power source, and it is being used more and more in all types of second homes. It is clean, convenient, free from odor, and gives the most uniform heat.

In figuring out the relative costs of different fuels, you have to take into consideration many more factors than simply the amount of heat provided per dollar. You should think of the installation cost, the efficiency of the fuel, and the insulation level of the house.

For instance, an electrically heated house must have twice the insulation thickness in the ceiling and the floor than that required by houses heated with fuel-burning systems.

Heating units vary in efficiency. Coal-heated steam and hot-water boilers operate at 60 to 75 percent efficiency; gas- and oil-fired boilers at 70 to 80 percent; forced-warm-air furnaces, gas-fired or oil-fired, generally about 80 percent;

oil-fired furnaces with pot burner, not over 70 percent.

Comparison of Fuels. *Wood* requires more labor and storage space than any other fuel. However, a wood fire is easy to start, burns with little smoke, and leaves little ash. For a vacation home, a wood fire is still the ideal type of heating system—if it provides enough heat.

Hardwood fuel that is well seasoned has about half as much value per pound as does good coal. A cord of hickory, oak, beech, sugar maple, or rack elm weighs about two tons and has the same heat value as one ton of coal.

Coal. Two kinds of coal are used: anthracite (hard) and bituminous (soft). Bituminous is most often used in homes. The heat value of different sizes of coal varies little. Vacation homes do not go in much for coal heat, although some cabins in very cold regions do.

Oil requires little space for storing or handling, and it leaves no ash. However, it is difficult to carry for great distances. It becomes an impracticable fuel to use in remote second homes.

No. 1 grade fuel oil is lighter and more expensive than No. 2 grade, but No. 2 gives higher heat value per gallon. An oil burner can be a vaporizing type or an atomizing type.

Vaporizers premix the air and oil vapor. Atomizers can be gun- or pressure-type, or rotary.

The gun burner is usually used in private houses; a pump forces the oil through an atomizing nozzle, where a fan blows air into the oil fog. An electric spark ignites the mixture, which burns in a refractory-lined firepot.

Gas can be used in the vacation home in al-

The vaporizing or pot-type oil burner is the least expensive unit to use for an oil-fueled system.

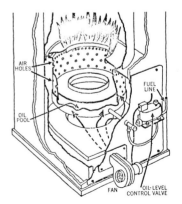

most any region of the country, since the fuel is either supplied by pipe, or stored in bottles. The gas is supplied to a burner head, where it is mixed with air for burning. A thermostat controls the gas valve.

There are three kinds of gas: natural, manufactured, and bottled. Bottled gas (usually propane) is called LPG (liquefied petroleum gas). This is the most commonly used type in vacation homes now.

All gas-burning equipment must be vented to the outside to avoid asphyxiation or explosion. All chimneys and smoke pipes must be kept free from leaks. Gas-burning equipment must be cleaned, inspected, and adjusted every year.

Bottled gas is heavier than air. If it leaks into a cellar, it will accumulate at the lowest point and create the hazard of an explosion. If you use bottled gas, make sure that the safety control valve is so placed that it shuts off the gas to the pilot as well as to the burner when the pilot goes out.

Electricity. Electric heating requires no chimneys or vents and gives a convenient, clean, even, safe heat. But your house must be as well insulated as possible and weather-stripped, with double- or triple-glazed windows. Insulation, vapor barrier, and weatherproofing should be planned in any new vacation home to provide the proper housing for an electric heating system.

Chapter 14

UTILITIES

THE vacation home of the old days, which had no running water, light, or heat, is practically extinct today. Even in the most remote spots of the country, electric power is usually provided by a public utility company. Naturally there are areas where there is no power to be had. Be sure to check into the power supply available when you shop around for a vacation site.

On the other hand, there are plenty of places in the country that do not have water readily available, and not all of them are desert areas. Many mountain spots do not have water for household purposes; the same is true of many flatland areas.

However, while the lack of electric power is not that serious, for you can always make use of some other source of power, water is absolutely essential. Fortunately, it can usually be obtained by digging a well. Water can be found almost anywhere if a well is dug deep enough.

ELECTRICITY

This is the age of electric power. Nuclear power stations are a thing of the present and the future. In a few years, every remote place in America may well be within range of a nuclear power source.

If power wires are close to the site of your vacation home, all you have to do is call up the utility company and order a lineman to hook you in. If the power wires are in the area but are not near your building site, you may have to have lines strung to bring in the electricity. But it costs money to sink poles in rough terrain. Poles are usually spaced about two hundred feet apart, and you can figure the cost of bringing power onto your site at about 50¢ a foot over ordinary landscape, plus about $50 per pole. If the distance is less than two hundred feet, hooking you in will probably be free.

Generator/Alternator. If you need power but cannot get it, you will have to create your own supply system. There are several machines capable of producing electric power. The simplest is the old-fashioned generator.

Generator. The typical generator runs on gasoline and can service a moderate-sized vacation house. It will supply about 2,700 watts of power for about $500, or 3,500 watts for about $600.

If you do not need to power anything but lights and refrigerator—that is, if you use some other type of fuel for cooking and heat—then you can

use a smaller generator, which supplies about 1,500 watts at less than $400.

Alternator. A new development in this field is the alternator, a brand-new approach to the production of electric power. The advantage of the alternator is that it is lighter, has fewer parts, and is more reliable than the generator. The alternator costs about $600 for a model supplying 3,000 watts.

The greatest problem with making your own electric power is that the machinery needs a great deal of maintenance and simply cannot be left to itself for long periods of time. You also have to count in the cost of gasoline to power the machine.

GAS

There is a way to heat and light a vacation home without electricity, of course, and that is to use LPG, liquid-petroleum gas, which is usually propane. You can have LP gas tanks delivered by truck to your site on a regular seasonal basis, and you can stock as many as six

The generator shown provides 3,500 watts of power, adequate to run an average-sized second home. The typical generator runs on gasoline, but some can be run on liquid petroleum gas or other fuels.

100-pound tanks, so that you always have a reserve when a tank runs out.

Liquid-petroleum gas will give you fuel for all the general needs of the vacation home: light, fuel for cooking, and heat for the house. You can also use LP for running a pump.

WATER

Although your vacation home may be located on the bank of a sparkling stream, you may be well advised not to use the water for drinking. Actually, the best source for water—aside from the pipes of a utility company operating in the area—is a ground water source like a well or spring. Surface water from streams, lakes, and ponds is always suspect—and can be dangerous to drink.

A properly located and constructed well is the best source of water for your own personal use. Well water is less likely to be contaminated than water from other sources. However, it may contain dissolved minerals such as iron and manganese that make it unpotable.

Quality of Water. Water for the vacation home must not possess bacterial or toxic-chemical content. Not only that, it should not contain excessive amounts of calcium or magnesium. In other words, good water should be "soft," rather than excessively "hard." Hard water makes bathing, cooking, and laundering difficult.

Silt suspended in water makes it look cloudy. Too many dissolved minerals, gases, or decaying organic matter may give it a bad taste and odor.

It is almost mandatory, if you are settling in

a fairly pristine site, to have the water tested for bacterial content and have it approved before using it. Your local health officer can advise you regarding the tests that should be made. He may even evaluate the results himself. Do not use water for personal use unless it has been approved.

How Much Water? In a vacation setting, each person in the family uses from about thirty to seventy gallons of water a day, which includes drinking water and water for sanitation requirements. Your water source should produce at least the minimum daily requirement for each member of your family.

If the water source produces only a minimal amount of water, you may need a storage tank or cistern to build up extra supplies of water for use during peak periods.

Wells. A well may be dug, drilled, bored, driven, or jetted. All but drilled wells are limited to loose, easy-to-penetrate ground formations containing few large rocks. Special equipment and skill are required to drill a well. Be sure the well driller you hire has a good reputation. Do not choose a well-drilling contractor on the basis of his low price. A higher-priced driller may give you a better well than the cut-rate man. He may drill deeper for better-quality water, and he may do a better job of sealing the well against contamination once it is dug. He may also use a better grade of casing in the construction.

For mutual protection, draw up a written agreement with the well driller, covering general construction specifications, costs, and payment

This cross section of a dug well shows how the shaft looks inside the ground. The protective layer of concrete extends down ten feet to ensure complete watertightness of the upper walls.

arrangements. (See Chapter Eight on dealing with architects and contractors.)

Location. The well should be located above and as far as possible from known or possible sources of contamination. Choose a spot that will make it easy for you to maintain and service the well. If you want your well next to a building, place it at least two feet beyond the drip line of the eaves.

Dug Well. The average dug well can be constructed either with hand tools or power tools. It penetrates to a depth of 50 feet or less, with a diameter of 3 to 20 feet. It is not practicable to dig a well through dense igneous rock. All other formations—clay, silt, sand, gravel, cemented gravel, boulders, soft sandstone, and soft fractured limestone—are acceptable.

The dug well can be cased as tightly as any other type of well. Concrete wall rings 3 feet

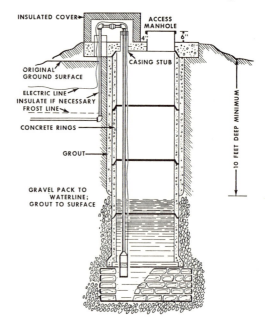

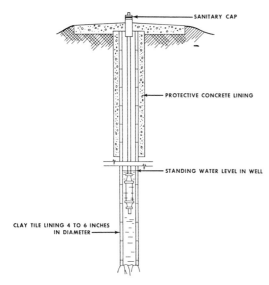

in diameter and 2 feet in length are usually used for casing, although other sizes are in common use. The well hole is made 12 inches larger in diameter than the well ring, and the upper part of the space is filled with concrete.

Bored Well. A bored well is constructed with either hand augers or powered augers. A hand-bored well is usually 8 inches or less in diameter; a power-bored well may be as large as 3 feet in diameter.

The bored well is usually cased all along its length for efficient service.

Driven Well. A driven well consists of sections of pipe coupled together with a well point and a water screen at the end. The point is driven down into the ground until the screen is below the level of the water table. Water enters the pipe through the screen.

The diameter of a driven well is about 1¼–2 inches; it can be drilled to a depth of 50 feet.

Drilled Well. Special well-drilling equipment

As can be seen by the drawing, bored wells are similar to dug wells, but are usually deeper and smaller in diameter.

is needed to construct a drilled well. It can go through rock formations.

Two types are used: percussion equipment, which is a cable tool; and rotary equipment, using both conventional and reverse-rotary methods. The difference is mainly technical, dictated by the type of rock formation involved, the diameter desired, the quantity of water needed, and the depth of the well.

The drilled well used to produce household water usually has a diameter of 6 inches or so.

Jetted Well. For sandy soils, a jetted, or hydraulic, well is the best to use. The hole for a jetted well is made by the force of a high-velocity stream of water directed into the ground where the well is desired. The water loosens the material and washes the finer particles upward and out of the hole. A jetting tool—bit or point—is then pushed down through the loose material.

How to Avoid Contamination. A well must be protected from every type of ground-surface contamination. All well casing must be durable and watertight and the space between the well casing and the sides of the well hole should be sealed with a watertight cement grout to below the "zone of contamination," so that water cannot drain down around the casing.

The zone of contamination is usually determined by the type of soil formation through which a well is drilled. It is the portion of soil that is subject to normal entry by surface flooding.

The upper casing terminal should have a watertight seal or cap. The terminal should be at least two feet above flood level. It is best to enclose the top casing in a pumphouse to keep the water clean if it is at all possible.

Disinfection. Before you draw water from a new well to analyze it for purity, you should disinfect the entire water-supply system to kill any bacteria introduced during construction or installation of the plumbing.

Here are the steps to take to disinfect a well:

1. Open the well and pour a gallon of chlorine bleach into it. Calcium hypochlorite tables can be used as an alternative.

2. Connect a garden hose to the well and draw water out through it until you can smell the strong odor of chlorine.

3. Flush the inside of the well casing thoroughly with chlorinated water. Wash the well cap or well seal.

4. Draw water through each faucet and outlet in the house until you smell a strong odor of chlorine. Turn the water off.

5. Let the water stand in the pipes 8 to 12 hours. Do not use any water during that time.

6. After 8 to 12 hours, run water through all the outlets until there is no more chlorine odor.

7. Do not forget that heavily chlorinated water may kill grass or shrubbery.

Pump. If you have dug a well, you must now have a pump to lift the water out of the ground and into the house. One of the most efficient methods of bringing water up from a well is an electric pump.

The cost of running such an electrically operated water system is trivial. For only one cent an hour, a pump will deliver more water than a man can pump by hand in the same time. More time and energy have been wasted in vacation homes in the past on hand pumping than on any other chore.

SUBMERSIBLE PUMP

Water Level. The depth and type of well you have determine the type of pump to use.

If the water in the well lies less than 22 feet below the pump, plan to use a *shallow-well jet* or *shallow-well piston pump.*

If the water level is more than 22 feet from the pump but less than 90 feet, use a *deep-well jet* or *deep-well piston pump.*

If the water level is more than 90 feet deep, use a *deep-well piston* or *submersible pump.*

Follow the manufacturers' recommendations on depth limits when they vary from the limits given above. Do not use jet, or submersible, pumps if the water you are drawing contains sand.

Pressure Tank. A pressure tank is a device that allows you to draw a small quantity of water without turning on the pump. It also helps to even out the flow of water during pumping operations.

The most commonly used pressure tank is a 42-gallon size. You can use about 8 gallons of water between the stopping and starting of the pump. A pressure switch attached to the tank provides automatic control of the motor and pump.

Pump Capacity. The capacity of the pump should not be greater than the capacity of the well to supply water. If the water flow is strong enough, choose a pump that will deliver 300 gallons of water per hour. This will enable you to use a 3/4-inch hose for fighting fires and watering gardens.

A 600-gallon-per-hour pump with special hose

and nozzle is recommended by some fire-protection agencies for effective fighting of small fires or for protecting adjacent buildings during a larger fire.

You will want a pump to deliver most of the water needed in a few short peak periods during the day. Select a size that will furnish the entire daily water needs in two hours or less of actual pumping time.

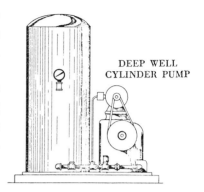

DEEP WELL CYLINDER PUMP

Appliances. Once the basic water-supply system has been installed, you can add many labor-saving appliances to your second home: a water heater, an automatic washing machine, a dishwasher, and a garbage-disposal unit.

Cost. Facilities and equipment represent the main cost of any water system. If a suitable well is available, the total cost of pump, pressure tank, and initial pumping may be as low as $250. Operating costs are minor.

SHALLOW WELL PUMP

Water Quality. A number of problems other than the presence of bacteria can affect well water: hard water, red water, black water, an off-taste, acid water, and turbidity.

Hard water is caused by an excess of calcium, magnesium, or iron, in the form of bicarbonates, sulfates, or chlorides. The condition leaves scaly deposits in pipes and water heaters. It also affects laundering adversely by requiring an excess amount of soap to produce soap suds.

Red water is caused by an excess of iron or manganese, or iron bacteria, in the water. The condition causes red stains to appear on clothing and porcelain plumbing fixtures. It also produces

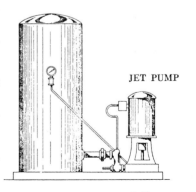

JET PUMP

a metallic taste in the water, makes a red slime appear in the toilet tank, and causes faucet water to turn a rust color after exposure to air.

Black water is caused by an excess of hydrogen sulfide gas, sulfate-reducing bacteria, or sulfur bacteria in the water. Silverware turns black, fine black particles appear in the water, and iron, steel, and copper parts of pumps, pipes, and fixtures corrode. Worst of all, the water takes on the definite taste of rotten eggs and even smells like rotten eggs.

Off-taste is caused by an extremely high mineral content with organic matter present, and excessive combined-chlorine residual in the water. The water tastes bitter, brackish, oily, or salty, or has a chlorine odor or taste.

Acid water is caused by carbon dioxide, or, in rare instances, by mineral acid—sulfuric, nitric, or hydrochloric. It causes metal parts on pump, piping, tank, and fixtures to corrode. It also causes red stains to appear on galvanized pipes and blue-green stains on copper or brass.

Turbidity is caused by silt, sediment, small organisms, or organic matter in the water. The water has a muddy or dirty appearance.

Treatment of Bad Water. Treatment to improve the sanitary quality of water or remove bacteria is called disinfection. Chlorination is the method most commonly used for small private water systems and the one usually recommended by public health authorities.

Chlorine is a good disinfectant and oxidizing agent. In sufficient concentration, it will kill coliform bacteria and disease organisms, reduce the bad tastes and odors of decaying vegetation, and oxidize sulfur, iron, and impurities of various types.

To chlorinate water, you need a chlorine solution, a container for it, and a chlorine injection device commonly called a chlorinator.

Ordinary laundry bleach can be used for disinfecting small water systems. One gallon of bleach is enough to give 5,000 gallons of water a chlorine dosage of 10 parts per million, which is deemed safe for human usage.

Stronger compounds containing up to 70 percent available chlorine can be bought to disinfect larger water systems. For instance, calcium hypochlorite is used frequently in tablet or powder form for this purpose.

Chlorinators. Chlorinators come in four types: positive displacement, suction, aspirator, and tablet.

Positive displacement. The positive-displacement chlorinator consists of a simple electric, diaphragm-type pump. It injects a fixed volume of chlorine solution into the water. An alternate type injects the chlorine solution into the water as it flows through the chlorinator.

Suction. The suction chlorinator consists of a chlorine control unit and a single line running from the chlorine container through the control unit to the suction side of the pump. The suction draws the chlorine into the water.

Aspirator. The aspirator chlorinator has no moving parts and does not require electricity for operation. Water flows through a venturi tube, creating suction that draws the chlorine solution into the water supply.

Tablet. The tablet chlorinator consists of a

container with hypochlorite tablets or a granular compound. Some water from the water supply bypasses through the container, forms a chlorine solution, and then flows back into the water supply.

Methods of Disinfection. To disinfect water you can boil it, pasteurize it, use ultraviolet light, or sterilize it with ozone.

Boiling can destroy bacterial contamination. Boil water vigorously for at least two minutes to ensure safe water. Sterilization kills all organisms. Disinfection reduces the concentration of organisms to safe levels. Protect all cooled water from recontamination.

Pasteurization is usually not practical for water. This process calls for heating the water to a temperature of 140–145 degrees Fahrenheit for at least ten minutes.

Ultraviolet light wavelengths have a highly germicidal effect. However, color, turbidity, and organic impurities in the water interfere with the transmission of ultraviolet energy and reduce the efficiency of the process to unsafe levels.

Ozonation is not a practical type of disinfection for vacation-home systems.

Water Softeners. Calcium and magnesium and sometimes iron in water make it "hard." The best way to soften hard water is to run it through a water-softener unit connected with the water-supply line.

A water softener consists of a tank containing an ion-exchange material, usually zeolite or resin beads. When the water passes through the zeolite or resin beads, hard calcium and magnesium ions are exchanged for soft sodium ions and the water is softened.

Iron Removers. Iron in ferric form occurring in water will stain clothes and plumbing fixtures. Ferric iron results when ferrous iron in well water is exposed to the air.

Four types of iron-removal equipment are available: water softeners, polyphosphate feeders, iron-removal filters, and chlorinator filters.

Water softeners. Zeolite will remove up to 10 ppm (parts per million) of soluble iron from water.

Polyphosphate feeders can handle up to 3 ppm of iron in solution. A phosphate compound coats the soluble iron and prevents its oxidation when the water is exposed to air.

Iron-removal filters. An iron-removal filter will remove up to about 10 ppm of iron. Much like a water softener, it contains a bed of natural or synthetic manganese greensand. Manganese dioxide furnishes oxygen to oxidize the iron, and most of the iron-oxide particles are filtered out in the lower half of the bed. Acid waters below a pH of 6.8 will pick up manganese.

Chlorinator filters. A chlorinator-and-filter unit chlorinates and filtrates through a sand or carbon filter to remove any quantity of iron in any form. The chlorine oxidizes and precipitates the iron, and the filter strains out the particles.

Neutralizing Acid Water. Acid water corrodes the metal parts of water systems—the pumps, piping, water tank, water heater, and fixtures. It also prevents the complete oxidation of iron in water. The acidity must be neutralized for effective removal of iron. Water having a pH of 7 is neutral. Below 7, the water is acidic; above 7, it is alkaline.

Objectionable Tastes and Odors. Hydrogen sulfide may be removed from water by chlorination followed by filtration through an iron-removal filter. If only small amounts are involved, use an iron-removal filter by itself.

Most objectionable tastes and odors, except a salty taste, can be removed by running the water through an activated-charcoal filter, commonly called a taste-and-odor filter.

Algae are a cause of bad taste and odor in pond water. Local health authorities will tell you how to control algae.

Turbidity. Muddy or cloudy water in excess of 5 ppm is objectionable for aesthetic reasons. If the rate exceeds 10 ppm, the water is probably not good for your health.

Filtration removes turbidity. If it is not completely effective, use a prefiltration treatment to reduce the amount of turbidity before the water reaches the filter.

Use a slow sand filter for treating pond water. This consists of an 18-to-24-inch bed of fine sand on top of a 6-inch layer of coarse gravel. The water moves through the filter at a rate of 3 gallons per hour per square foot of filter bed area—or about 72 gallons per day.

You can use powdered gypsum to treat pond water. Spread it over the surface of the pond at a rate of 12 pounds per 7,000 gallons of water. Use an aluminum-sulfate solution for treatment in a tank, feeding in the aluminum-sulfate solution into the tank with an alum feeder.

Aeration of Water. You can improve the quality of water by the simple process of aerating it. Spray it into the air, allowing it to cascade over steps, passing it through beds of coarse coke or stone, or bubbling air into it.

The benefits of aeration include:

1. Elimination of bad tastes and odors from the water.

2. Oxidation of the ferrous iron in water, helping to remove iron.

3. Increase in the oxygen content of oxygen-deficient water.

4. Improvement of the taste of flat water.

Chapter 15

SANITATION

Another important consideration for the vacation homeowner is sanitation. Most vacation areas lack public sewage disposal and depend on individual systems for effective sanitation.

If your site is not accessible to public sewage disposal, you will have to plan your own. A septic tank is the most common method presently in use. It is fairly inexpensive and operates satisfactorily with a minimum of maintenance.

SEPTIC SYSTEMS

The average septic tank is a large, watertight underground vault, usually made of concrete or coated metal. Waste from the household empties into this tank. Bacterial action then decomposes and liquefies the waste, and the sewage flows into a disposal field made of drain tile or per-

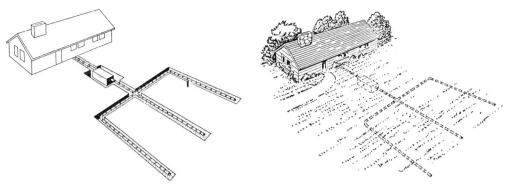

forated pipe, where it spreads out into the soil. The tile or pipe is laid in trenches or in a seepage bed and is covered with soil. The soil is planted with grass, so that no part of the system is visible. In the earth, soil bacteria and air render the sewage harmless.

In an ordinary septic-tank absorption field, the drain tile is laid in trenches, as pictured in the first illustration (above left). The trenches are then filled in with soil (above right), and the entire area is planted with grass or ground cover, so that nothing is visible above ground. The sewage is carried by the field to all parts of the yard. The cross-sectional illustration (below left) shows how the sewage seeps out through the porous tile and is then absorbed and filtered by the surrounding soil. To substitute for an absorption field, a seepage bed (below right) can be dug if the yard area is not large enough for a good absorption field.

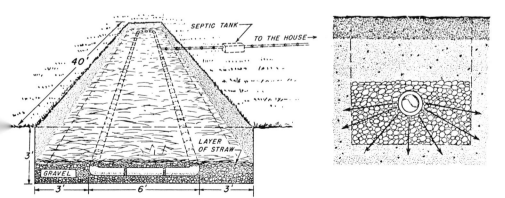

The average-sized septic system in use today is a 750-gallon unit. This unit requires cleaning out once every two to five years. The installation of such a septic system runs about $600, including the tank and the disposal field. A field for a tank of that size would include about two hundred feet of open-joint clay pipe.

Do not place a septic tank any closer than fifty feet from a well or cistern. The disposal field should be at least 100 feet from a well or cistern.

It is not a good idea to place a septic tank under a driveway. The heavy weight of a car or truck may crush both the tank and the field.

A lakeside vacation site usually slopes toward the water, and local ordnances forbid a disposal field that drains in that direction. Faced with such a problem, you may have to pump sewage to a permitted disposal area that lies in a direction away from the lake.

In some septic systems, a disposal field is not used but is replaced by two or more leaching pits. A leaching pit is a circular hole about five feet in diameter and five feet deep and lined with a concrete cap at the top. The top is constructed to lie a foot below ground level.

Cesspool. A cesspool is an old-fashioned type of septic tank that has more or less gone out of fashion. It is still used in beach areas, however, because the sandy soil allows for rapid drainage of sewage. Moreover, a beach-house cesspool may receive sewage only part of the year, and so needs to be pumped out only occasionally.

Soil-Absorption Capacity. A good septic system

can function well for many years if it is properly installed and maintained and if the soil in the disposal area has a satisfactory absorption capacity. If the soil is not satisfactory, the disposal system will work improperly, no matter how well constructed and installed it is.

Therefore, the first thing to do in planning a septic-tank sewage disposal system is to find out if the soil on your property can easily absorb liquid sewage—called effluent—that flows from the septic tank. Generally, sandy soils absorb effluent rapidly, clayey soils, slowly.

The efficiency and durability of your sewage disposal system depends largely on the absorption capacity of the soil. If the soil does not satisfactorily filter and absorb the effluent, unfiltered sewage may reach the surface and contaminate the ground water. Unfiltered sewage that reaches the surface gives off a stench and attracts flies and insects. Fly-breeding areas can be the source of disease.

The absorption capacity of the soil helps determine the size of the sewage disposal field. A soil with a slow rate of absorption needs a large field. If the soil has a slow rate of absorption, you may need a field larger than your lot. And some soils may not be suitable for use as absorption fields at all.

Why Fields Fail. A sewage absorption field can fail to work properly when the soil is poorly drained or is so compact that the absorption rate is too slow for the amount of effluent involved.

A poorly drained soil becomes saturated with water during wet weather. There is no space left for septic-tank effluent. An absorption field may function well in dry weather but fail in wet weather for that reason.

If the soil has a slow absorption rate, effluent may rise to the surface even in dry weather. In wet weather the field will turn into a bog.

If the land is too steep, it may cause the absorption field to fail, too. The field may fail also if the water table is too high, if there is only a shallow layer of soil over bedrock, if there is a cemented layer of soil below the trench bottom, or if the area if periodically flooded.

Soil Factors. How well a septic-tank sewage system works depends upon the rate at which effluent moves into and through the soil. This is called soil permeability.

Other soil characteristics may affect permeability: ground-water level, soil depth, underlying material, slope, and proximity to streams or lakes.

Soil permeability is the quality that enables water and air to move through soil. It is determined by the amount of gravel, sand, silt, and clay in the soil, the *kind* of clay involved, and other factors. Water moves faster through sandy and gravelly soils than through clayey soils, as would be expected.

Certain clays expand little when wet; others are very plastic and expand so much that they shut off the pores of the soil. This slows water movement and likewise reduces the capacity of the soil to take in septic-tank effluent.

Ground-Water Level. Some soils lie over pockets of moisture, where the ground-water level lies only a foot or a few feet below the surface of the soil the year around. In other soils, the ground-water level is high only in winter and early spring. In still others, the water level is high during rainfall. Under any of these conditions, a disposal field will not function properly.

If the ground-water level rises to the tile or pipe of the disposal system, the soil becomes saturated and cannot absorb effluent. This causes the surface of the soil to become a foul-smelling, unhealthy bog.

Rock Formations. For good absorption, there should be at least four feet of soil material between the bottom of the trenches, or seepage beds, and any rock formations. In an area where water comes from wells and the underlying rock is limestone, more than four feet should separate the two to prevent unfiltered effluent from seeping through the cracks and crevices in the limestone layer.

Different Kinds of Soil. If a site contains different kinds of soils, the absorption capacity may not be affected at all, provided the different soils have about the same absorption capacity. But if they are different, the absorption capacity may be seriously diminished.

In a case of this kind, try to distribute the effluent to the various types of soil separately, so that each soil can absorb and filter according to its proper capacity.

Slopes. A slope of less than 15 percent does not create a serious problem in the construction or maintenance of an absorption field. However, on a sloping soil the trenches must be dug on

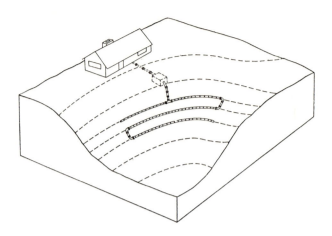

the contour of the slope, so that the effluent flows slowly through the tile or pipe and disperses properly over the field.

On a steeper slope, it is difficult to lay out and construct the absorption fields. Control of the flow of effluent may be a real problem. Improperly filtered effluent may reach the surface at the base of the slope, and wet, contaminated seepage spots can result.

If there is a layer of dense clay, rock, or other impervious material near the surface of a steep slope—especially if the soil is sandy—the effluent will flow above the impervious layer to the surface of the slope and run unfiltered down the slope.

For severely sloping land, over 15 percent, the septic-tank sewage disposal system must be laid out in a different fashion from flat-land installation, as shown.

Percolation Test. The best way to determine the absorption capacity of the soil on your vacation site is to take a percolation test. Such a test will also aid in calculating the size of the absorption field necessary to take care of the effluent of your sewage system.

Most local regions require trained personnel

to make percolation tests. Such a test follows these steps:

1. Dig six or more test holes 4 to 12 inches in diameter and as deep as you plan to make the trenches or seepage beds. Space the holes uniformly over the proposed absorption field. Remove any smeared or slick surface soil from the sides of the hole. Remove loose dirt from the bottom of the holes and add 2 inches of sand or fine gravel.

2. Pour 12 inches of water in each hole. Add water as needed to keep the level exactly 12 inches above the gravel for at least a period of four hours, or preferably overnight during dry periods of weather. If the percolation test is made

This is a cross-section of a percolation-test hole. The other test holes can be seen distributed over the field in the background.

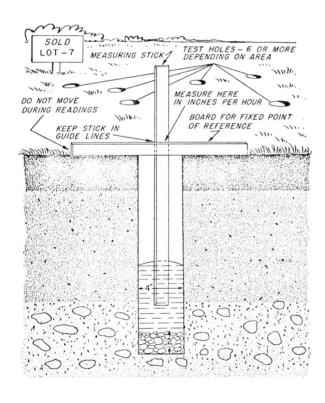

during the dry season, wet the soil thoroughly to simulate its condition during the wettest season of the year. The results should be the same regardless of the season in which the test is made.

3. If you are testing overnight, adjust the water level to about 6 inches above the gravel. Measure the drop in water level over a thirty-minute period. Multiply that by 2 to get the number of inches of sinkage per hour. The resulting figure is the percolation rate. After getting the percolation rate for all the test holes, estimate the average.

4. If no water remains in the test holes overnight, add water to bring the depth to 6 inches. Measure the drop of the water level every thirty minutes for four hours. Add water as often as needed to keep it at a 6-inch level. Use the drop in water level to calculate the percolation rate, figuring inches of sinkage in thirty minutes.

5. For sandy soils, where water seeps rapidly, reduce the time interval between measurements to ten minutes and run the test for only one hour. Use the drop that occurs during the final ten minutes to calculate the percolation rate.

6. Make percolation tests of seepage pits in the same way. You must test each contrasting layer of soil. Use a weighted average of the results to figure out the size of pit you need.

Calculating the Size of the Absorption Field. After determining the percolation rate of the soil, you can now calculate the size of the absorption field you need to make your septic-tank system work.

To calculate the size of the absorption field needed, you must first find the percolation rate of the soil. Then consult the chart to get the square feet of absorption area needed per bedroom. Multiply this figure by the number of bedrooms, and you have the total square feet of absorption area needed.

Count the bottoms of the trenches as the effective absorption area. To find how long the trenches should be and how much drain tile or perforated pipe is needed, divide the square feet of absorption area needed by the width in feet of the trenches. This figure gives you the total length of the trench.

The trenches should be spaced 6 to 8 feet apart. Multiply the total trench length by the distance between the trench center lines to get the total area in square feet to be occupied by the absorption field.

Sample: Two bedroom house. Trenches 24 inches wide.

Soil percolation rate is 2 inches per hour. The chart shows the required absorption area per bedroom to be 250 square feet. The absorption area equals 500 square feet divided by 2 feet (the trench width). That equals 250, the total length in feet of the trench and tile or pipe required.

The best layout for a system like this would be four trenches, each about 62 feet long. Three trenches about 84 feet long would also suffice. Do not make trenches over 100 feet in length in any case.

Seepage Beds. To estimate the size of a seepage bed, determine the size of the absorption field needed in square feet. Count the entire bottom of the bed as the effective absorption area. For

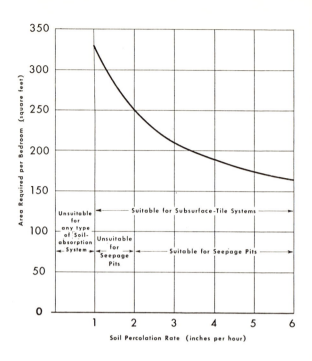

Chart shows the size of absorption field needed for a private residence in the country. (Adapted from Manual of Septic Tank Practice.)

a two-bedroom house, if the soil percolation rate is 2 inches per hour, you need 500 square feet of seepage bed. A seepage bed 10 feet wide and 50 feet long or a bed 12 feet wide and 42 feet long will meet the requirements.

Seepage Pits. To calculate the size of a seepage pit or pits needed, determine the size of the absorption field, as explained above. Count only the vertical walls below the inlet as the effective absorption area of a seepage pit; do not count the area on the bottom of the pit. Divide the total square feet of the absorption field by the depth of the pit in feet. This will give you the circumference of the pit; divide the circumference by 3.14 to get the diameter of the pit.

Site for Septic Tank. Soil samples vary so much from place to place that it is not practicable to give any specific rules for the use of soils as absorption fields for all localities. Local health regulations also vary greatly.

Before planning your sewage disposal system, familiarize yourself with the health regulations of your community, the permit and inspection requirements, and the penalties that may be imposed for violations.

Be sure to confer with the city or county planning commission, the local health department, the extension specialist, the engineering or agricultural department of colleges and universities, and the state board of health.

In selecting the site for your sewage absorption field, keep in mind the following points:

1. Soil permeability should be moderate to rapid. The soil percolation rate should be at least 1 inch per hour.

2. Ground-water level, during the wettest season, should be at least 4 feet below the bottom of the trenches in a subsurface-tile absorption field and 4 feet below the pit floor in a field using seepage pits.

3. Rock formation and impervious layers should be more than 4 feet below the bottom of the trenches, the seepage bed floor, or the pit floor.

4. It is difficult to lay trenches and seepage beds on slopes steeper than 15 percent. If steep, shallow soils underlain by rock or impervious material are used as fields, the septic effluent is likely to seep to the surface.

5. Never select a site for an absorption field within 50 feet of a stream or body of water. Never

install a sewage disposal system on a plain that is subject to flooding.

6. Where different kinds of soil occur very near each other in an area where you want to dig a sewage absorption field, have a detailed inspection made of the site and then distribute the effluent to each kind of soil separately. Do not use the site if the soils differ greatly in absorption capacity.

A soil survey can help you select a site that is suitable for a sewage absorption field.

Man-made patio area blends in beautifully with nature's own landscaped foliage. Large, spacious wooden deck has been carried out from the wall of the vacation home here, with a combination railing-bench built in as structural part of deck.

Chapter 16

LANDSCAPING

THE old-fashioned cabin in the woods never needed complicated landscaping to make it fit in with its environment. But the modern vacation house usually will be improved by effective landscaping.

No matter what kind of relationship exists between house and surrounding foliage, the structure itself must fit snugly into its environment. It should seem to be as permanent an object on the landscape as the trees and shrubs. A vacation house that has been well landscaped will have a certain permanence to it. A badly landscaped vacation house will look as if it had been dropped down on a bare strip of ground without any forethought or preparation.

Since a house is a man-made structure, it tends to be angular and composed of straight lines set at right angles to one another. Natural growth tends to produce soft, informal lines—circles, curves, arcs, and combinations of these. Nature itself tends to neutralize the starkness of machine-made lines.

Trees and shrubs help a building blend in with the ground on which it sits. Plants of all kinds—trees, shrubs, and ground cover—give a house the impression of rest, of harmony, and of belonging to earth and sky.

But man-made lines as well as nature's can help make a vacation site more dramatic, more exciting, and more attractive. Garden trellises, decks, fences, patios, and all sorts of extensions of the house help to blend in house and terrain.

Of the two types of landscaping—natural and man-made—the one to begin with is the one nature has already provided you: the ground, the site, and what grows on it.

NATURAL LANDSCAPING

Interest in ecology and in the relation of man to his environment has stimulated a new concept in landscaping: the natural look. The natural look in landscaping emphasizes the blending of the house with its natural environment—the use of rocks where they exist, the use of sand or gravel where it lies, the growth of plants indigenous to the region.

The modern garden in a natural landscaping situation accentuates the original ecological conditions. You plant shaded areas with shade-loving growth, rather than cut trees to eliminate the shade or force sun-loving plants to grow there. You plant hot, dry areas with sun-loving growth indigenous to the area. You leave a natural slope as it is or plant it with ground cover instead of laboriously reshaping it into a flat area for a lawn. You leave trees where they grow unless there are too many of them and you have to thin them out.

Low maintenance is the key word in dealing with plants and trees that grow within the periphery of the vacation home. You want your house to give you leisure enjoyment, not a life of grassmowing, flowertending and treetrimming.

Essentially, small flower beds and raised borders of plants will be the best thing for you to use as elements of a vacation house garden. Small garden areas planted with bright annuals and set off by rock borders or brick walls will break up the monotony of ground cover or virgin woodland.

If the location of your house calls for the use of a rock garden, you can always plant succulents like cactus in its many varieties amid the rocks and then add groups of sun-loving plants.

Pots and Planters. Two of the most versatile and useful types of gardening equipment for the vacation house are the flower pot and the planter.

Use annual flowers in pots for quick bright blooms. If your house has a raised deck, you can place potted plants anywhere on it. If you have an uncovered overhang of trellis, you can hang baskets with bright blooms from it.

The planter is a large version of the pot and is simply a square box made of wood—usually redwood or cedar—fitted with casters for easy rolling. It is filled with dirt, in which plants grow

This eye-catching planter box enhances the airy atmosphere of an entry deck and helps create an attractive natural setting for outdoor living.

singly or in groups. A planter can be shifted from one end of the patio or garden to the other as the sun moves in its daily course.

Foundation Planting. The vacation home does not usually need foundation plants of any kind, but if you do decide to use them, it is advisable to carry out the rough texture of natural growth that surrounds the house.

Rhododendrons, azaleas, viburnum, and mountain laurel are excellent. Other broad-leaved evergreens and needle-leaved evergreens will keep their shape all year long and will blend in well with the exterior siding of the house.

Ground Cover. A vacation home differs considerably from the average suburban home in that it usually does not have a large expanse of grass surrounding it. Ground maintenance should be kept at a minimum in a second home. Use ground-cover plants rather than grass for the effect of the natural environment.

The best of these ground covers are fine substitutes for grass. They help give texture to the grounds around a house—and in that way tend to blend in the living terrain with the manufactured house.

Ivy is an excellent ground cover; so is pachysandra, creeping myrtle (periwinkle or *Vinca minor*), dichondra, and many other types, like euonymus and sedum.

Trees. In the woods, of course, you do not have to think about planting trees. They are already there. In a barer landscape, however, you will need to plant some specimens. There is nothing so beautiful and warmly inviting as a vacation home surrounded by sheltering trees.

You will get better results from planting year-round trees—evergreens—than those that shed their leaves in the fall. If deciduous trees are already there, however, leave them, and add some evergreens.

Pines, firs, junipers, and cedars can be used not only as low bordering walls and as dividers, but they can be shaped the same way a hedge can be shaped.

If you need shade, use a medium-sized flowering tree that will provide bright color during the spring and good shade during the hot summer days. A dogwood is a decorative tree, and it is not too large. A gardening center near your vacation site will have specimens of various decorative shade trees on display.

This design is patterned after the Japanese engawa, which links rooms opening onto court or garden and brings the foliage of garden or woods right into the living area.

There is one important thing to remember about planting trees. Most people trying to bring shade and green to a bare area have the tendency to overplant. Try to curb that tendency. Plants always seem to grow bigger than you think they will.

Trees that you buy at a nursery are carefully selected as to growth habits; the final height and size of each one can be accurately predicted. Do not buy a tree that will grow seventy feet tall if you want one with a height of only thirty feet.

In the woods, nature has taken care of the selection of growth. Usually, a forest will contain a large number of certain kinds of trees, with several aliens among the more numerous types in order to balance the scene. Nature tends to design its woods beautifully by not mixing too many different kinds together.

Do not buy a hit-or-miss selection of many differing kinds of trees. Buy several of the same kind or shape or variety, to be used as accents here and there. Leave variety and high color to the planters and pots that you can control. A tree is a permanent natural background fixture of a landscape and cannot be moved about at will.

General Tips on Landscape Planting. When you plan any kind of natural landscaping arrangement for a vacation home, pay attention to these important tips:

1. Use only plants that will thrive in your geographical and climatic area.

2. Use shade-loving plants in the shade; use sun-loving plants in the sun.

3. Pay particular attention to the plant's preference for acid or alkaline soil.

4. Do not forget its growth habits or size or its life expectancy.

5. Make your planting look natural.

6. Keep the center of any yard area open so that the eye will be drawn to the distant border—the effect achieved will be one of space and harmony.

7. Do not crowd together shrubs, flowers, and trees. Spread them out.

8. Arrange plants in groupings: masses of flowers of the same color; several shrubs of a kind; trees in pairs.

9. Buy plants only from reliable sources, so that you can count on proper performance from each plant.

MAN-MADE LANDSCAPING

Almost any outdoor addition to a vacation home should be considered a part of the whole and should be planned to fit in with the over-all landscaping picture. Since a vacation home is designed to be used during the best months of the year and since it is set up for leisure and outdoor life, the surrounding terrain of the house is most important.

Patio. Outdoor construction for the vacation home usually involves to a large degree the living area immediately adjacent to the house. That area is usually set aside for outdoor eating, drinking, lounging, and entertaining.

It is referred to by different terms in different parts of the country. In the East, and in England, it is sometimes called the terrace. In the West it is called the patio. In various parts of the country it is called the deck. It can be called the loggia, the stoop, the veranda, the lanai, and so on.

Both "terrace" and "patio" are accurate terms, describing something slightly different. A terrace is a flat portion of land that adjoins the house; a patio is a flat portion of land that adjoins a house and may be walled in; a deck is a flat structure that is attached to the house or built out from it.

Whatever it is called, the patio is the central portion of outdoor living for millions of people who have vacation or second homes.

It is in effect a party room, a living room, and a playroom all rolled into one—outdoors. Being an extension of the indoor living area, it takes the working load off the inside of the house.

The patio is also the final phase of landscaping that blends the house with its natural surroundings.

Choosing a Site for the Patio. The location of the patio is of utmost importance. It can be either at the back of the vacation home, on the side, or even in front. Choose a site where you have plenty of land and a good view. Do not forget that the prevailing wind must be considered, too, along with the position of the sun and its path from morning to night.

When you decide on the layout of your vacation home, plan outdoor and indoor areas together—with your architect or builder if you have

Double-deck level here creates living area outdoors along the side of the house, providing a level space for family living and entertaining on the leisure home's sloping site.

A flat yard gets a lift from U-shaped deck of Douglas-fir 2-by-4's, breaking up all-one-level look. Pond scooped out in center of deck flows under closed end of U, adding pleasing natural mood. Note patio levels of natural lawn (1), concrete slab at bottom of deck steps (2), and mulched garden corner for variety of surfaces (3), in addition to wooden decking (4).

one, or with your family if you are doing it alone.

The patio should be easily accessible from the house. One approach to it should be from the kitchen area, because a great deal of eating will be done outdoors. Another approach should be from the master bedroom, for that cup of coffee first thing in the morning and that nightcap before going to bed.

Surfacing. The essential part of any patio is its surfacing. It can be, as the terrace is in England, of well-tended, mowed lawn grass. It can be composed of crushed gravel or of smooth, washed creek stones, it can be a poured concrete slab attached to the house or it may be simply composed of pounded dirt. It may even be a

leveled site covered with crushed seashells.

The modern patio, however, is usually made of wooden decking material, of sand and gravel, of flagstones laid in concrete grout or sand, of concrete squares or rectangles laid in sand, or of bricks laid in sand or mortar.

You can obtain bricks at any building-supply house, and can then lay them in any pattern you wish. The same is true of concrete squares or rectangles and flagstones.

The first step in laying brick surfacing is to level the ground on which the bricks are to rest. Then spread a layer of sand over the level ground. Lay the bricks on top of the sand, fitting them tightly together. Concrete squares can be laid in the same manner.

Flagstone laying is a tricky business, because of the odd shapes of the stones. The best way to proceed with flagstones—after laying a level bed or sand—is to piece out the ultimate pattern by fitting the flagstones together on top the sand. Start with the big flags, and use the small ones to fill in between, chipping off any corners that overlap.

These materials are hard and shed water well. You can easily maintain the patio by watering it down with a hose. Be sure to make your surfacing with a slight pitch, so that water will drain away from the house.

Decking. A patio may be termed a "deck", because in many cases its surface is made of wooden decking. Wooden decking is used in the vacation home for many different purposes.

The primary use is as a substitute for the traditional porch of the urban or suburban

The house on this spectacular panoramic site, was inaccessible until a deck-type bridge was installed. Now the bridge is one of the outstanding features of this all-redwood structure.

house. It can be elevated fairly high over the ground and is frequently built extending out from the garage or the second floor. It can also be placed below earth level and laid in the dirt. Preservatives are available to keep such wood from rotting.

The advantages of decking are many: it is attractive, it is useful, it is easy to work, and it sheds water and snow and ice without difficulty.

A unique advantage of a wooden deck is that it can make an almost impossible building site accessible. That is, on a steep site, a deck can be built as a kind of bridge from the hill to the house. A deck can also be extended out from the house over a slope for a spectacular view that would not be possible without it. The deck can "make" such a house.

Where to Put It. The true deck is an integral part of a home. The surface is an extension of the floor inside the structure.

The railing along the deck must be strong enough to support the weight of several people leaning against it. If the deck is placed high above ground, it is a good idea to have extra protection along the railing. If children will use the deck, you can erect wooden screens along the railing to keep them from falling over the edge.

The location of the deck is as important as the siting of the house itself. The deck should be on a level with the inside floor, or just a bit below it. Do not locate the deck too far below the floor—one step down is really too much. An inch or two is the ideal difference.

A cantilevered deck, if it is properly designed and constructed, gives the viewer the impression of hanging out in space while he is sitting and enjoying himself in comfort.

Size. Never confine yourself unduly to size when you plan a deck. The larger the deck is, the better and more interesting and serviceable it will prove to be. A huge deck can make a small house worth living in.

In fact, in outdoor locations where the weather is usually good—on a lake site, at the seashore—deck area is the most desirable space, suitable for sunbathing, resting, and sleeping. Because it is very much like a room of the house, the deck should be large enough to hold a number of people and chairs and lounges and tables. No deck should be less than eight feet in any one direction.

Construction of Deck. A deck can rest on the ground, it can extend out from the house itself, or it can be supported by piers or piles from the ground or water. It is usually made of timbers that are fastened together by underpinnings of some sort.

Foundation requirements, load limits, and building regulations always apply to decking and must be followed in construction. A collapsed deck can be a very serious matter. Laws have been passed to prevent faulty construction in decks.

If the deck is going to be high and the terrain is hard to negotiate, you must hire a professional landscape architect or contractor to do the job for you. The deck must be designed and built in accordance with the requirements of local codes.

Composition of Deck. The deck is composed of two parts: the platform and its supports.

The *platform* of the deck is made up of timbers that rest on joists, which in turn are supported by beams. The beams usually rest on concrete footings or wooden pilings.

Usually the *footings* and *pilings* must extend into the earth to undisturbed soil or below the frost line in cold climates. In low decks, the beams may rest directly on the footings. Concrete blocks or precast footings seated firmly in the soil can be used. On beach property, where the sand constantly shifts, concrete footings can be bypassed in favor of pile-driven posts or telephone-pole-type columns.

The most spectacular type of decking is that which is cantilevered out from a house, with no diagonal supports. Actually, the joists for the deck are the same as those used for the floor of the house inside. In long spans, steel beams can be used for cantilevered structures. The weight of the house itself counterbalances the extended deck.

Material. For decking material there is a wide choice of woods: redwood, Douglas fir, Engel-

Special entry court creates an outdoor room for leisure living, with sun trellis, benches, deck, gate, and fence all constructed of natural-finish wood.

mann spruce, Idaho white pine, lodgepole pine, sugar pine, ponderosa pine, Western larch, and Western cedar.

The wooden supports between deck and earth must be treated with pentachlorophenol or creosote to guard against rot and termites. Those that rest on concrete footings can also be treated, but water will drain off the concrete and cause less trouble to the wood.

Posts are fastened to concrete footings by means of a special metal fitting inserted into the concrete while it is drying. The decking itself is laid with small spaces between the boards to permit quick drainage of water.

Platform lumber for decks usually consists of 2-by-3's, 2-by-4's, or 2-by-6's in the woods mentioned above. Space supports are about 4 feet apart, if 2-by-6's are used, or 2-by-3's or 2-by-4's laid on edge. Space supports are about three feet apart if 2-by-4's are laid on the face.

Face-laid 2-by-4's or 2-by-6's should be placed with the bark side up. You can determine the bark side of a piece of wood by checking the arch of the ring marks at the top of the board. The boards are laid not more than a quarter of an inch apart. This gap will allow for enough drainage and will not catch women's high heels.

Use hot-dipped galvanized or stainless-steel nails and fastenings; otherwise, rust stains will ruin the wood and weaken the structure.

Deck Shape. The deck itself can be any shape you want it to be. The conventional shape is, of course, rectangular or square. However, a deck can be free-form, if you like. It can surround trees growing through it, or it can encircle or skirt a special focal point in a yard.

There are a number of interesting decks pictured in this chapter to give you an idea of the scope of design possible for this type of manmade structure.

Fences. The vacation site far removed from other vacation sites has a sense of privacy that is priceless. Leisure, relaxation, and recreation are dependent on this sense of privacy—a remove in space from the stress of civilization.

If you are settling in a vacation area that is also the site of many other homes, you may have to use your landscaping skills to secure your own personal privacy.

Your patio may extend out from your vacation home right up to the property line of your neighbor's house. It is at this point that you will have to try to create your own privacy by erecting a fence or by growing a hedge.

It is generally acceptable to use fencing in a vacation site to cut off your view of your neighbor. Simply build the fence along the perimeter of the patio. The size of the fence can be determined by how much of the neighbor's house you want to hide.

A mixture of hedge trees *and* fencing is the ideal answer to this landscaping problem. By planting trees next to board fencing, you can conceal or camouflage the fence.

You can build the fence as high as local ordinances allow—heights usually of 6 to 8 feet. You can also make a good screen out of plywood panels. The most attractive fences, however, can be made from wood of all kinds: redwood, cedar, Southern pine. The fences themselves can be

built in many popular designs: board on board, shadow box, basketweave, post and rail, and so on.

Landscape Architect. If you can afford a professional landscape architect, by all means hire one to fix up your vacation site. Check your local chapter of the American Society of Landscape Architects. You can ask his rates and find out whether or not you can afford him.

For a flat fee, he may come to discuss ideas with you—not only for your patio, deck, and fencing, but also to recommend plants for natural landscaping.

He may even contract the labor and supervise the project to completion for a percentage of the total expenditure.

This simply constructed fence of heavy wood posts shows what can be done with ingenuity and originality.

Chapter 17

WINTERIZING

Unless your second home has been designed and built for year-round living, there will come a time in the fall when you will have to close it up for the winter months. Winterizing a vacation place applies not only to homes in the mountains and in cold areas, but also to those by the seashore and lakeside.

The point in winterization is to close down the house and protect the furnishings and objects inside it—not only from wintry blasts and storms, but from thieves and marauders. Not only can human marauders harm a house, but animals can as well.

There is no particular order in "battening down the hatches" of the second home, but you should pay special attention to certain zones: outdoors, indoors, doors and windows, kitchen, bedroom and living-room furnishings, utilities and so on.

For each area there are certain things you should do—and some things you should *not* do.

OUTDOORS

Beginning with the outdoors, look around carefully to see what you can and cannot leave outside during the winter months. If you have a deck with furniture on it, you should remove all the mobile furnishings and take them inside. Such mobile furnishings include planters, pots, hanging baskets, barbecue equipment, badminton nets, lights, and whatever else is not built in or anchored to the ground or house.

Built-in benches and built-in trellises need not be removed unless they are apt to be damaged by high winds, ice, or snow. You will have to use your common sense here. The main idea is to secure everything outdoors so that it is left in a condition to withstand high winds, sleet, snow, ice, and flooding.

If you have a beach cottage, you will have little worry over snow, but you should concern yourself with blowing sand and high water.

Be sure that the locks on the doors and windows are in perfect order. Security is a very definite problem in a second home that is left unguarded for months on end.

Doors and Windows. Remove all screens from doors and windows from the outside and store them somewhere inside the house.

Grease all the hinges, levers, and openers on the windows to keep them from rusting during the winter months. If your vacation home is near the sea, greasing is a definite must each season.

Close all windows and doors and lock them from the inside wherever possible. If there is any likelihood of heavy winds, nail stripping across the bottom and top of every door to keep sand out of the house. If any of your windows are loose in their frames, protect them similarly.

In some cases—such as a vacation site on a windy beach or plain—you can tack sheets of plastic over windows and doors on the outside to help keep the house sealed.

If there is drapery of any kind on your windows, close it to cover the glass. This will prevent splinters of glass from flying inside the room if the panes should be broken in a high gale.

INDOORS

Once the outdoors is in order, you can then move inside to prepare the house itself for the winter. There is something to be done in each room. The following list includes most of the more important things that should be done before closing the house.

Bedroom and Living-Room Furnishings. Strip all beds and bunks down to their mattresses and store the bedding and spreads either on hangers in a closet or in a clothes box of some kind.

In order to prevent moisture damage to the material, place layers of paper between each thickness of bedding. The paper will absorb the moisture.

Leave the dresser drawers open a half inch or so. The circulation of air in the furniture will help prevent the contents from becoming mildewed.

Move everything away from the windows; broken glass can seriously damage furniture. Whenever possible, place furniture against an inner wall, away from outside walls. Move all upholstered pieces out of any direct line of sunlight. Sun blazing in a window can fade upholstery very quickly.

Bathroom. Remove any liquids subject to freezing from the medicine cabinet in the bathroom. It is also a good idea to remove any drugs from the medicine chest. Thieves who break into houses are always on the lookout for drugs of any kind.

Kitchen. Plan to remove everything edible in the kitchen. Any food left in the house will be sure bait to lure insects, rodents, and vermin of all kinds. Do not leave candles or soap out in the open. Store them in a tightly closed metal can. Grease in any form also attracts rodents and vermin. Store all spices, flour, sugar, and other nonperishable staples in tinned containers with tight lids.

Do not leave bottles of carbonated beverages in the house. Freezing temperatures will burst the bottles and leave sticky liquids all over the floor. Remove any wines or liquors; these items are prime targets for thieves and housebreakers.

Clean out the refrigerator thoroughly. Wash it with soap and water, and then rinse it. Prop open the door slightly, so that air can circulate freely. Also let air move through the freezing compartment. Do not forget to unplug the refrigerator from the wall outlet.

Your Valuables. Gather up everything in the

house that is movable—portable television, transistor radios, cameras, projectors, stereo equipment, records, portable typewriter, and anything else that is valuable—and either lock it up in a completely safe place in the house or take it with you. Frankly, it is always best to take such appliances with you. Security cannot be completely depended upon in any second home.

Rugs. Take up all rugs and carpets that are not permanently attached to the flooring. Clean them and then store them in a storage closet or attic crawl space.

Be sure that the storage place is above the floor level; these materials will mildew and rot if subjected to moisture.

Floors. After the rugs and carpets have been removed and the furniture has been piled in the corner, clean all the floors carefully, and then wax and polish them.

A good coat of wax will protect the finish from excess moisture, cold weather, and any other hazards of winter. Also, when you move back in the house in the spring, you will not have to start out with the backbreaking job of waxing and polishing the floors.

Fireplace. Be sure the damper is closed in a wood-burning fireplace. If you fail to close it, rain will come right down into the fireplace itself. So will sleet and snow.

Also, birds will tend to fly down into the chimney to make their nests inside and will find an opening into the house. Chipmunks and squirrels may discover a way in to the house through the chimney, too, along with other rodents.

In order to double-protect yourself against such an invasion of animal visitors, cut a piece of plywood the size of the chimney top and fasten it in place. This will keep out animals as well as rain and snow.

Water. Shutting off the water supply in a second home is one of the most important and most necessary moves to be made in closing down the house for the winter.

If your house is connected to a public water supply, turn off the water main first. You will probably find the main outside somewhere, usually near the road. If your home has a main valve inside, turn the water supply off there.

Then, with the water supply shut off, turn on all the faucets and drain out the water left in the pipes until there is none left.

If the winters in the area are very hard, remove the water even from the toilet and the drain traps beneath the sinks. Simply pump it out of the toilet; each trap beneath a basin usually has a pet cock to control the water. If the winters are relatively mild, it probably will not be necessary to drain these fixtures.

In the event that your water supply comes from a private well, disconnect the pump and shut off the supply of water at the main valve. Then proceed as above.

If the heat in your home is supplied by water or steam baseboard heat, you must drain that water out of the pipes. This is an extremely complicated procedure and must be done by a heating or plumbing expert.

Utilities. At the very last minute, have all the utilities cut off: telephone, garbage collection, electric power, gas, newspaper, and any other service you may have.

The trick here is to time the utility shutoff with the moment you intend to leave the house.

OPENING UP

If you have taken care of winterization in the manner suggested, it will be no problem at all to come back to the house in the spring.

The first step is to have all the utilities turned on and to restock your food supplies.

Next, open all the doors and windows, reattach the screens, and let fresh air into the house.

Chapter 18

FINANCING AND INSURANCE

FINANCING the purchase of a second home or getting together enough money to buy materials and hire a contractor to build one has for many years been a rather difficult proposition.

Banks and lending institutions have been notoriously reluctant to lend money to people who want to establish a second home for themselves in some remote part of the seashore or mountains.

The fear of seeing the house wiped out in a flash flood, a hurricane, or some other act of God has prevented banks from acting impulsively—if banks have ever been known to act impulsively.

FINANCING

Within the past ten years, however, the situation has been changing for the better. At that time the first fully equipped vacation home came into being, replacing forever the flimsy loose-jointed "cabin" that heretofore was the rule rather than the exception in the wilds.

Since then, communities of vacation homes have been growing by the seashore, by the lakeside, and in many scenic parts of the mountains and prairies. Securing a loan and a permanent mortgage on a second home is no longer the unheard-of thing it was in the early 1960's.

Retirement Loans. One exception to this general rule has always been the retiree. If you were contemplating immediate retirement and were planning to purchase a house in which you and your family would be living the year around, you could always get Veterans Administration or Federal Housing Authority backing to purchase the house.

Even now you cannot get VA or FHA insurance on second-home loans, but your chance of getting a regular loan on the conventional lending market is good if your credit rating is A-1 and you have a good, solid income.

Cost of a Loan. Different parts of the country operate under a number of financial conditions, but, generally speaking, you can probably buy a second home these days by putting up 10 percent of the cost of the home, with a 7-8 percent initial charge for the first ten months.

When the house is completed, you can then get a 12-to-20-year mortgage on the house by providing a 25 percent down payment. The interest on the mortgage—the 75 percent balance—may run about ½ percent higher than a conventional loan on a year-round home in the same locality.

You will undergo a thorough, highly inquisitive credit-rating investigation, however, before the loan is finalized.

If you do not want to buy a lot and build a home in a vacation community, but want to search out an isolated mountain peak far from civilization, your chances of getting a good loan to build the house will shrink considerably. In fact, if you are searching for such a lot, do not spend any money on the real estate until you are sure that you can finance the building of the house.

It is quite probable that the moneylender may refuse to make a loan on a remote site. Banks and lending institutions do not like to put money into plots of land too far from the locality where the bank operates. Bankers like to keep an eye on their investments.

However, if you have a good, established credit rating with banks and lending institutions, you may be able to swing a loan. Most bankers are very shrewd and know good land values. If you can convince one of them of the value of the land you are interested in, and of its potential as a resalable property, he may let you have the money.

Different Kinds of Loans. You can get a mortgage loan from a bank, from a savings and loan association, from an insurance company, or from a mortgage banker.

There are three types of loans, two of which are applicable only to retirees desiring loans for year-round second homes: FHA-insured loans; VA-insured loans; and conventional loans.

The FHA Loan. An FHA mortgage loan is one insured by the Federal Housing Administration to protect lenders from losses in case the borrowers fail to pay.

To get an FHA-insured loan, you make a small down payment and obtain a mortgage through regular channels for the balance of the purchase price.

The mortgage loan is made by a bank, by a savings and loan association, by a mortgage company, by an insurance company, or by some other FHA-approved lender. An FHA loan is *not* a government loan; it is simply *insurance* to the lender against the borrower's failure to repay.

To qualify for an FHA-insured loan, the following FHA minimum standards must be met:

1. The house must be livable.
2. The house must be soundly built.
3. The house must be suitably located as to site and neighborhood.
4. The buyer must have a good credit rating.
5. The buyer must have the cash to close the mortgage.
6. The buyer must have a steady income to meet mortgage payments.

The application for an FHA loan is made to any FHA-approved lender, not to the FHA itself. The lender forwards the papers to the FHA insuring office, which reviews the buyer's credit history and appraises the property to determine the amount the FHA will insure.

If the FHA approves your application, you are so informed and you then arrange to borrow the money from the lender to close the deal. The FHA collects a mortgage insurance premium of ½ of 1 percent, on top of the regular interest rate.

The minimum down payment on new houses

is 3 percent of the first $15,000; 10 percent of the next $5,000; and 20 percent of the remainder, up to a maximum of $33,000. Most FHA-insured loans run 30 years, but they may also run for 10, 15, 20, 25, and sometimes 35 years.

The VA Loan. Veterans Administration loans, called GI loans, are mortgage loans guaranteed by the Veterans Administration. The VA itself does *not* lend the money to you, but it enters into an agreement with the lender to guarantee or insure a loan up to an agreed amount.

In other words, the VA insures the lender that he will not suffer any loss if you fail to reply the loan.

One advantage of a GI loan is that a home can be purchased with a very small down payment. In some cases, no down payment at all is required.

Other benefits are: an extremely low rate of interest on the loan; a long period of amortization; and a property appraisal by the VA, based on "rule of reasonable value."

There is no maximum amount for such a loan.

Both FHA-insured and VA-insured mortgage loans are available only on second homes built by individuals planning retirement living on a year-round basis.

The Conventional Loan. A conventional mortgage loan is simply a deal between a borrower and a lender, with no government guarantee to back up the lender. If you as a borrower default, the lender is stuck with the house.

At the same time, the lender can charge you whatever interest he can get, within limits; he can decide what construction standards are required; and he can determine the economic standards that qualify you as a buyer.

For the prospective buyer of a second home who is not contemplating retirement, the conventional mortgage loan is the only way to finance the house. But in many cases, the developer of a leisure community will be able to steer the buyer to a lending institution that will take care of him. Anyone wishing to build on his own can usually find someone who will finance his project.

The biggest holders of conventional loans are savings and loan associations. Some commercial banks, mutual savings banks, and life insurance companies, as well as pension funds, nonprofit institutions, credit unions, and real estate companies also make conventional loans.

Savings and loan associations usually require a smaller down payment than other lenders, but they may charge a slightly higher interest rate for affording you this advantage.

How to Get a Loan. As you can understand from reading the above, it is not easy to take out any kind of a loan, really. A bank always wants to check out your credit rating before making a loan, even a personal one. If you have a lot of outstanding long-term debts like payments on a refrigerator, car, or boat, you had better forget trying to secure another loan immediately, particularly a large one for a second home. You will need a grade A-1 credit rating to get it.

Then, once you have secured the loan, you will have to count on paying about $300 for closing costs. These costs may run somewhat higher or lower in different parts of the country.

Closing costs include the following:
1. A survey of the lot.
2. Termite inspection of the house.
3. An appraisal of the property and house.
4. A title search of the property to see that it is clear of encumbrances or liens.
5. Insurance on the house.
6. Recording of the deed.
7. Taxes on the property.
8. Hazard insurance for the property and house.

What a Loan Entails. Once the bank looks at the property and decides to lend money on its potential, it will *probably* give you a loan equal to 75 percent of the total cost of the house on a 10-to-20-year mortgage.

To pay this loan, they will charge 1 percent of the total amount of the loan and charge an interest rate a bit above the going rate for the average mortgage loan in the area.

However, a savings and loan association, or a large bank, *may* charge 2 percent of the loan, and an interest rate about 1 percent higher than the going rate for the area.

How to Finance a House. If you are unable to interest a bank or lending institution in lending the money for the second home you want to build, you may be able to resort to these alternate plans of financing:

1. You can refinance your first home with a second mortgage and use that money to build the vacation home. A second mortgage is a mortgage loan taken out against the equity you have already earned in your first home—that is, the amount of the capital you have already paid

off—but it is usually issued at a higher rate of interest than the first mortgage. You will have to pay back both the first mortgage and the second simultaneously, of course. This money is paid in one payment, however.

2. You can borrow on the cash-surrender value of any kind of life-insurance policy you own. You will have to pay back this loan in the same way you would have to pay back a second mortgage, of course, or forfeit the cash value of your insurance policy.

3. You can always go to a finance company and take out a loan. However, this type of loan always has a very high interest rate. And the interest for the entire loan for the duration of its existence is included in the amount borrowed. You will, in effect, pay about double the stated interest rate. If this is the only type of loan you can get, you have to pay the price for it.

4. You can always take out a personal loan at a bank. Then, with the money you get, you can buy or build the shell of the vacation home, as described in the early chapters of this book. On completion of the shell, you can then begin to finish off the inside. As soon as you have a substantial bit of equity in the incomplete house, you can finance the rest of the construction costs on the equity, or what has already been built and paid for.

Advantage of a Second Home. There are a number of advantages to owning a second house that have nothing to do with the enjoyment of your leisure hours. Here are a few of them:

1. Putting money into a second home is a method of enforced saving. In other words, you cannot spend the money you put into a building

project. The money turns into a piece of property that takes on value in its own right.

2. Building a second home diverts money into a place where it becomes a hedge against inflation. Money itself loses value with inflation. Property values increase with inflation. The dollar you put into your house is worth two dollars, while the dollar you put into your savings account is worth fifty cents (disregarding interest).

3. The interest you pay on a personal loan or a mortgage loan is deductable from your income tax.

4. If you can rent your second home to others during the time you are not using it, you can realize a substantial amount of income.

5. You can get a tax advantage out of an income-producing property, such as a rented second home, which is a saving in addition to the amount of money you take in from the property.

6. When you repair income-producing property, you receive a tax break on the repair bill.

INSURANCE

Although it is not the easiest thing in the world to take out an inexpensive insurance policy on a second home, it is possible. If you are satisfied with a particular insurance company that has policies on your house and your car, contact them if you are interested in taking out a policy on your second home. If you are a good risk, you are likely to get a good policy written for you.

Fire Insurance. Of utmost importance to the

owner of a second home is fire insurance. Fire can destroy any house in minutes.

The rates for fire insurance are generally low, although they do differ from place to place. They are determined by a schedule published by the National Board of Fire Underwriters. A number of factors govern fire insurance rates, according to the NBFU:

1. Availability and capacity of water supply in the area.

2. Manpower of the nearest fire department, if any.

3. Size and capacity of fire-department equipment.

4. Fire-alarm system in house.

5. Police protection and patrol.

6. Building codes in area.

7. Strictness of code enforcement in construction.

8. General geography of the homesite.

The structure of the house in question has an effect on insurance rates, too. The type of construction can make a difference.

The rates for frame construction are higher than the rates for masonry construction. As a matter of fact, some companies do not cover houses of frame or log construction, unless they have continuous-masonry foundations.

Extended-Coverage Endorsement. There is a secondary type of coverage that can be added to ordinary fire protection in a second home. This type of coverage adds protection against damage from a number of destructive elements other than fire: riots, civil commotion, explosions, aircraft, vehicles, smoke, windstorm (on a $50-deductible basis, for a larger premium), and hail (on a $50-deductible basis, for a larger premium).

Special Form and Broad Form. On a $50-deductible basis you can extend your policy to cover a number of other special cases: Glass breakage, falling trees, water damage from plumbing and heating systems, vandalism, malicious mischief, collapse, ice, snow, and freezing.

Special Form covers the house only.

Broad Form covers the house and its contents.

Endorsements. If you carry fire insurance on your first home, you may be able to have an endorsement written into your policy that will cover your vacation house with fire insurance along with extended coverage and special form and broad form mentioned above.

Also, if you have a personal-liability policy on your first home, you can have it endorsed to cover a secondary residence at about one third of the original cost again.

It is particularly desirable to have liability coverage if your second home is used a great deal, with the possibility of injury on your property to persons outside your family always there.

Cost of Insurance. The cost of fire insurance and extended coverage on your second home is fairly low when you consider what is involved in writing the policy.

A cabin or house in a remote area will cost more to insure than a structure in a populated colony, where there is organized fire and police protection all the year round.

APPENDIX

MANUFACTURERS OF PREFAB, PRECUT, OR MODULAR VACATION HOUSES

Ahonen Lumber Co., Pine & Mill Sts., Ironwood, Mich. 49938 [Modular]
Air King Mfg. Corp., Tigard, Ore. 97223 [Precut]
Aladdin Company, Bay City, Mich. 48706 [Prefab]
Allied General, Inc., 14200 S.W. 256th St., Princeton, Fla. 33171 [Modular]
American Timber Homes, Inc., Escanaba, Mich. 49829 [Precut]
Arbor Homes, Inc., 1261 Meriden Rd., Waterbury, Conn. 06720 [Prefab]
Barden & Robeson Corp., 235 North Ave., Penn Yan, N.Y. 14527 [Prefab]
Boise Cascade Corp., 13575 St. Charles Rock Rd., Bridgeton, Mo. 63044 [Prefab]
Broadmore Homes of Texas, Inc., 2800 E. Industrial, Waco, Tex. 76703 [Modular]
Burkin Homes Corp., White Pigeon, Mich. 49099 [Modular]
Butler Mfg. Co. (Canada) Ltd., 3455 Queen Elizabeth Way, Burlington, Ont., Canada [Prefab]
Certain-teed Products Corp., Valley Forge, Pa. 19481 [Modular]
Dead River Co., 55 Broadway, Bangor, Maine. 04401 [Prefab]
GBH-way Homes, Inc., Walnut, Ill. 61376 [Prefab]
Globe Industries, Inc., 2638 E. 126th St., Chicago, Ill. 60633 [Modular]
Great National Homes, 22 Melrose St., Boston, Mass. 02116 [Precut]
Hilco Homes Corp., 70th & Essington, Philadelphia, Pa. 19153 [Precut]
Hodgson Houses, Inc., 540 Madison Ave., New York, N.Y. 10022 [Prefab]
Home Building Corp., 303 N. Park Ave., Sadalia, Mo. 65301 [Modular]
Insilco Corp., 1000 Research Pkwy, Meriden, Conn. 06450 [Precut]

Intermodulex NDH Corp., 2 Corp Park Dr., White Plains, N.Y. 10604 [Prefab]
International Homes of Cedar, 260 California St., San Francisco, Calif. 94111 [Precut]
International Shelters, Inc., Americana Bldg., Houston, Texas 77002 [Modular]
K Products Corp., 4940 Montecito, Santa Rosa, Calif. 95404 [Precut]
Lewis Mfg. Co., 23rd & Michigan, Bay City, Mich. 48706 [Prefab]
Lindal Cedar Homes, Inc., 10411 Empire Way S., Seattle, Wash. 98178 [Precut]
Lumber Enterprises, Inc., Box 1211, Bozeman, Montana 59715 [Precut]
Magnolia Homes Mfg. Corp., Hwy. 61 South, Vicksburg, Miss. 39180 [Mobile]
Manassas Lumber Corp., 506 Centreville Rd., Manassas, Va. 22110 [Precut]
Manufactured Homes, Inc., 330 Kalamazoo St., Marshall, Mich. 49068 [Prefab]
Mid America Homes, Inc., Rte 3, Box 38, Crown Point, Ind. 46307 [Prefab]
Miller Mfg. Co., Inc., 7th & Stockton Sts., Richmond, Va. 23211 [Precut]
Monarch Industries, Inc., Box 441, Middlebury, Ind. 46540 [Modular]
Montgomery Builders Supply, 803 W. Main St., Grove City, Pa. 16127 [Prefab]
National Homes Corp., Earl & Wallace, Lafayette, Ind. 47902 [Prefab]
Nationwide Homes, Inc., 1100 Rives Rd., Martinsville, Va. 24112 [Modular]
New England Homes, Inc., Box 464, Porstmouth, N.H. 03801 [Prefab]
Norwood Sash & Door Mfg Co., Ross & Sectin, Cincinnati, Ohio 45212 [Prefab]
Pease Company, 900 Forest Ave., Hamilton, Ohio 45012 [Prefab]
Presidential Homes, Inc., Arney's Mount Rd., Pemberton, N.J. 08068 [Prefab]
Reasor Corp., 500 W. Lincoln St., Charleston, Ill. 61920 [Modular]
R-J Industries, Box 237, Readlyn, Iowa 50668 [Prefab]
Roycraft Industries, Inc., 117 First St., Chesaning, Mich. 48616 [Prefab]
S. B. C. Corp., Phillips Ave., Albany, Georgia 31705 [Prefab]
Shelter-Kit, Inc., 26 Franklin St., Franklin, N.H. 03235 [Precut]
Squires Mfg. Co., 609 County St., Milan, Mich. 48160 [Precut]
Stirling Homex Corp., 1150 E. River Rd., Avon, N.Y. 14414 [Modular]
Swift Industries, Inc., 241 Curry Hollow Rd., Pittsburgh, Pa. 15236 [Precut]
Tandy Industries, Inc., 525 S. Troost Ave., Tulsa, Okla 74101 [Prefab]
Timber-Lodge, Inc., 105 W. 18th Ave N., Kansas City, Mo. 64116 [Precut]
Walpole Woodworkers, Inc., 767 East St., Walpole, Mass. 02081 [Prefab]
Ward Cabin Co., Box 1298, Bangor, Maine 04401 [Precut]
Weston Homes, Inc., PO Box 126, Rothschild, Wisc. 54474 [Modular]
Westville Homes Corp., PO Box 1, Westville, N.H. 03892 [Prefab]
Wickes Corp., 110 W. A St., San Diego, Calif. 92101 [Modular]
Wisconsin Homes, Inc., 425 W. McMillan St., Marshfield, Wisc. 54449 [Prefab]

VACATION HOUSE PLANS

American Plywood Association, 1119 A Street, Tacoma, Wash. 98401
Home Building Plan Service, 2235 NE Sandy Boulevard, Portland, Ore. 97232
Western Wood Products Association, Yeon Building, Portland, Ore. 97204

INDEX

(Figures in italics indicate pages upon which illustrations occur.)

Access road, 22
Accessibility of house, 13, 16
Acrylic paint 207
A-Frame, 12, *42*, 42-5, *43*, 100, 130, 183, 184, *204*
Agreement, contractual, 150
Alkyd resin paint, 208
Alternator-generator, 241
American Plywood Association, 27
American Society of Landscape Architects, 286
Appliances, home, 182
  kitchen, *18*
Architect, 27
  hiring of, 135, 138, 143
  landscape, 286
Asphalt roofing shingles, 197-8, *197*
Awning window, 177

Baseboard-heat unit, 235
Bay window, 177
Bevel siding, 190
Board and batten, 51, 184, 190, *193*
Bow window, 177
Box-beam ceiling, *15*
Brand names, 142
Bridge to home, 22, *280*

Budget, construction, 141
Build, best time to, 59
Building codes, 27
  tips, 158-82
Built-ins, 223-227
Bungalow siding, 190
Burners, heater, 236
Butterfly roof, *197*

Cabin, mountain, 8, 10, 60-4, *61-4, 67, 100*
Camp, mobile-home, 110
  selection of, 117, *118*
Cape Cod house, 184, 185, 189
Carpentry, 54
Casement window, 176
Cedar, 51, 75, 78, 81, 83, 131, 188, 189
  shakes, 184
  white, 75, *75*
Ceiling, 204, *204*
  heat, 235
  tiles, 203
Cement blocks, 122
Ceramic tile, 203
Cesspool, 258
Chalet, cedar, 131, *132*
  Swiss, *132*, 184

307

Chlorinators, 251
C.I.T. Financial Services, 113
Closets, how to build, 227
Coal (fuel), 237
Colonial doors, 173
  siding, 190
  style, *203,* 184-5
Color toning, 215
Combination doors, 175
Community living, 13, 14, 22
Concrete aggregate wall, 166
  block construction, 166
  continuous foundation, 161
  running, 122
Construction, concrete block, 166
  costs, 13, 22, 28
  crib, 167
  custom, 135-57, *144, 145*
  "finish," 91, 99
  interlock, 69-84
  log, 167
  "mechanical core," 91
  modular, 127-34
  precut, 53-68
  prefabricated, 85-106, *88, 89*
  "rough finish," 90, 97
  sectionalized, 127
  "shell," 53, 54, *61,* 89, 90, 92, 162
  stone wall, 166
  when to build, 59
  wood-frame, 167
Consumer Credit Protection Act, 115
Contemporary architecture, 185
  doors, 174
  styling, 185
Contractor, building, 52, 143, 146-50
  dealing with, 156
  selecting, 148, 199
Contractual agreement, 150
Core, mechanical, 87
Cost factor, 29
Cottage, 97, 131, 184, 185, 189
Countryside house, 2, 6
Crib construction, 167
Curtains, *15*
Custom construction, 135-57, *144,* 145

Deck, 33, 188, *268, 277, 278,* 279-285, *280*
  construction of, 282
  material for, 282
  post-and-beam, 50
  shape of, 284
  site of, 277
  size of, 281
Desert home, 7, *150, 151*

Design, expandable, 59
Door, storage, 223
Doors, 172-5
  Colonial, 173
  combination, 175
  contemporary, 174
  Dutch, 174
  folding, 174
  patio, 175
  sliding, *15,* 174
  traditional, 173
Double-hung window, 175
Drainage, 13, 19
Drawers, how to build, 225
Drinking water, 242
  see also water
Drop siding, 190
Ducts and grilles, 233

Electric heating, 235
  power, 18, 238, 240
Erosion, soil, 9, 13, 19
  sand and rock, 3
Expandable design, 59, 63
  home, 32-7

Farmers Home Administration, 115
Fences, 285, *286*
  rail and post, *123*
FHA (Federal Housing Administration), 111, 115, 295, 296-7
Fields, septic, 259
  calculating size of, 264-5
Financing, 13, 14, 16, 294-304
  cost of loan, 295
  means of, 300-1
  mobile home, 113
  retirement loan, 295
Finish, "natural," 215
Finished prefab, 87, 91, 99
Finishing off, 179
Fire insurance, 302-3
Fireplace, *21,* 22, 50
Fitting (carpentry), 55
Flood damage, 3, 5, 19
  insurance, 4
Floor, concrete slab, 162
  painting of, 217-8
  wooden, 163
Flooring, 179, 200-3
  block, 164
  ceramic tile, 203
  oak, 201
  Old English Plank, 201, *202*
  parquet, 202
  Ranch Plank, 202, *202*

resilient tile, 202
strip, 164
surfaces, 201-3
tongue and groove, 201
wood, 201
Flora and fauna, 13, 23
Foundation, 22, 23, 158-61
  planting, 272
Franklin stove, 17, 49, 230
Fuels, heating, 236-8
  coal, 237
  electricity, 238
  gas, 237
  LPG (liquid petroleum gas), 238, 241
  oil, 237
  wood, 237
Furnace, pipeless, 231
  central, 235

Gable roof, *196*
Gambrel roof, *197*
Gas, 237, 241
Generator, 18, 240
Glass doors, sliding, *15*
Ground cover, 272

Hardboard, ceiling *204*
  exterior: board and batten, 196, *196;* horizontal lap, 195, *196;* reverse batten, 196, *196;* shingle and shake, *196;* and wood-grain designs, 196
  interior, 200-1
Hardwood floor finishing, 217-9
Heat, 228-38
  pump, 235
Heaters, 231-5
  baseboard radiator, 234
  baseboard unit, 235
  ceiling, 235
  central furnace, 235
  combined heater and cooler, 232
  ducts and grilles for, 233
  efficiency of, 236-7
  forced warm-air, 232
  furnace, pipeless, 231
  gas-fired, 231
  humidifier, 233
  oil-burner, *237*
  perimeter-loop system, *232*
Heating systems, 230-6
  electric, 235
  hot-air, 230
  hot-water, 233
  steam, 233
High-wind damage, 3

Hip roof, *197*
Home Building Plan Service, 148
Hot-air heating, 230
Hot-water heating, 233
Houses, vacation
  A-Frame, 12, *42,* 42-5, *43,* 100, 130, 183, 184, *204*
  cabin, mountain, 2, *8,* 9, 10, 60-4, *61-4, 67, 100*
  cluster, *35, 37, 39,* 40, *41*
  cottage, 97, 131, 184, 185, 189
  countryside, 2, 6
  desert, *150, 151*
  expandable, 32-7
  lakeside, 5, 8, *140,* 187
  lodge, 65, *66, 67,* 68, *68, 78,* 184
  log cabin, 69-84, *72, 73, 74,* 75, *75, 79*
  plains, *187*
  ranch, 184, 185
  roundhouse, 47, 48, *49*
  saltbox, 102, *103,* 104, 124
  seaside, 2, *4, 66,* 68, *103,* 144, *145, 149, 280*
  snow and ski, 12, *187, 190*
  stone, 166
  Swiss chalet, *132,* 184
Humidifier, 233
Hurricane damage, 3

Ice-storm damage, 9
Inspection, final, 152
Insulation, 228
Insurance, 302-4
  broad form, 304
  considerations, 27
  cost, 304
  endorsements, 304
  extended coverage, 303-4
  fire, 302-3
  mobile home, 125
  special form, 304
  water damage, 4
Interior styling, 198
Interlock construction, 69-84

Lakeside home, 2, 4, 5, 8, *140, 187*
Lamp, kerosene, 17
Landscaping, 182, 269-86
  architect, 286
  decks, *277,* 279-85
  fences, 285
  foundation planting, 272
  ground cover, 272
  man-made, 276, *283*
  mobile-home, 120, *120,* 124

309

pots and planters, 271, *272*
tips on, 275
trees, 273
Landslide damage, 9, 11
Latex paint, exterior, 207
  interior, 213
Leasing land, 11
Loans, 296-300
  FHA, 296
  how to secure, 299
  VA, 298
Lodge, 65, *66, 67,* 68, *68, 78,* 184
Lodgepole logs, 71
Log cabin, 69, *72, 73, 74,* 75, *79*
  construction, 167
Logs, precut, 70
  laminated, 78, 79, 80
  lodgepole, 71
  modelogs, 72
LPG (liquid petroleum gas), 238, 241

Mansard roof, *197*
Masonry, 166
  paint for, 212
Materials, building, cost of, 28
Measuring (carpentry), 55
Mechanical core, 87, 91
Mediterranean villas, 203
Metallic surface, how to paint, 212
Mildew-resistant paint, 208
Millwork, 180-2
  baseboard, *180*
  battens, 181
  casing, 180
  chair rail, *181*
  closet rods, 182
  corner guards, 181
  cornice, *181*
  hand rails, 181
  quarter rounds, 181
  trim, *180*
  wainscot caps, *181*
Mobile home, 107-126
  cost, 114
  extras, 122
  financing, 113
  interior, *110*
  landscaping, 120, *120, 124*
  size, 111, *112*
  park: selection of, 117, *118*
Modular construction, 127-134, *129, 133*
  home, *129,* 130, *133*
Module, 127, 128, *129*
Modules, plywood, 31
Mountain cabin, 2, *8,* 9, 10, 60-4, *61-4, 67, 100*

NAREB (National Association of Real Estate Boards), 25
"Natural" finish interior paint, 215
  color toning, 215
  finish, 215
  light stain, 216
  multicolor spatter, 216
  oil stain, 215
  stain, 215
  stippled, 216

Oak plank floor, 201
Oil (fuel), 237
Oil-base paint, exterior, 206-7
  interior, 213
Old English Plank floor, 201
On center, 31

Paint
  exterior (house paint): acrylic, 207; alkyd resin, 208; latex, 207; oil-base, 206-7; and water-base, 206-7
  floor, 217-8
  how much to use, 212-3
  interior: latex, 213-4; oil-base, 213; and water-base, 213-4
  masonry, 212
  metallic surface, 212
  shingles and shakes, 210
  stain, 208
Painter, subcontractor, 221-2
Painting, 182, 205-22
Paneling, plywood, 179, 198-9
  conventional, 179, 198-9
Park, mobile-home, 110
  selection of, 117, *118*
Parquet floor, 202
Patio, *268,* 276
  site of, 277
  see also deck
Payment terms (home), 149-52
Percolation test, 262, *263*
Piers and jacks (mobile home), 122
Pine, lodgepole, 71, 189
  southern, 51, 189
  white, *74, 75*
Plains house, *187*
Plan, house, 27, 142, 151
Planters, 271, *283*
Plywood construction, 26-52, 171
  grades of, 192
  house of, 30
  exterior, 191
  interior, 198-9, *200*
  prefinished, 200, *200*
  painting of, 209
  siding, 191

surfaces, 51, 171, 192-5
see also siding, plywood
Precut construction, 53-68
  logs, 70
Prefabricated construction, 85-106, *88, 89*
  "finished," 91, 99
  "mechanical core," 91
  "rough finish," 90, 97
  "shell," 90, 92
Prefinished paneling, interior, 51, 86
Pollutants, 17
Post-and-beam deck, 50
Posts, wooden, foundation, 159
Pressure tank pump, 248
Property, how to buy, 25
Pump, 17
  heat, 235
  pressure tank, 248
  water, 247
Purlins, 50

Radiator, baseboard, 234
  convector, 234
Ranch house, 184
  style, 185
Ranch Plank Floor, 202
Real estate agents, 25
Real estate, how to buy, 25
Recreational facilities, 8
Redwood, *8,* 50, 51, 101, 188, 189
Refuse collection stand, 124
Resilient tile, 202, 203, *203*
Right-of-way, 16
Road, access, 22
Rock, 9
Roof, 196
  butterfly, *197*
  gable, *197*
  gambrel, *197*
  hip, *197*
  mansard, *197*
  pitched, *12*
  shed, *196*
Roofing shingles, 197
  asphalt, 197
  cedar, 197
Room divider, how to build, 225
Rough-finish, 86, 90, 97
Roughing-in, 178
Roundhouse, 47, 48, *49*

Saltbox house, 102, *103,* 104, 184
Sanitation, 256-268
Seaside house, 2, *4, 66, 68, 103, 144, 145, 149, 280*
Sectional assembly, *94*

Sectionalized construction, 127
Security measures, 13, 19
Seepage pits, 266
Septic system, 256
  absorption field, *257, 262*
  calculating size of, 264-5
  cesspool, 258
  fields, 259
  percolation test, 262, *263*
  why fields fail, 259
Settlement, final, 153
Sewage, *18*
Shaping (carpentry), 55
Shed roof, *196*
Shell construction, 53, 54, *61,* 86, 90, 92, 162
Shelving, how to build, 226
Shingles and shakes, *12,* 50, 171, 189, *190, 211*
  applying wood preservative, 211
  painting, 210
Shiplap siding, 190
Siding, 184, 190, 191
  materials for: concrete block, 166; crib, 167; hardboard, *196*; log, 167; masonry, 166; milled wood, 167-70; plywood, 171; and shingles and shakes, 171
  patterns of: bevel, 190; board and batten, 190; bungalow, 190; channel rustic, 190; Colonial, 190; drop, 190; shiplap, 190; and tongue and groove, 190
  plywood, surfaces: brushed, 194; channel groove, *193*; fine line, *193*; kerfed, 194; and MDO channel groove, 195
  MDO reverse board and batten: reverse board and batten, 194; rough-sawn, 194; striated, 194; and Texture 1-11, *192*
Site, building, how to select, 1, 13
Skirting (mobile home), 123
Slab, concrete, 162
Sleet damage, 9, 11
Sliding window, 176
Snow damage, 9
Snow and ski house, 2, 11, 12, *187, 190*
Specifications, architectural, 151
Stain, 208
  light, 216
  opaque, 209
  penetrating, 209
  shingles and shakes, 210
Steam heating, 233
Steps (mobile home), 123
Stone, *21,* 22

foundation, 160
   house, 166
   wall, 166
Storage shed (mobile home), 124
Stove, Franklin, 17, 49, 230, *231*
Strip flooring, 164
Studs, 31
Styles, architectural, 183-204
   Cape Cod, 185
   Colonial, 185
   contemporary, 185
   ranch, 185
   traditional, 185
Styling, exterior, 186, *187,* 191
   interior, 198
Swiss chalet, *132,* 184

Terms of payment, 149-52
Terrace, 217
   see also patio
Terrazzo tile floor, 203
Texture 1-11 (plywood surface), 171, *192*
Tidal conditions, 3
   damage, 5
Tie-down anchors (mobile homes), 124
Tile floors, 202
   ceramic, 203
   resilient, 202
Tongue and groove floor, 201
Traditional doors, 173
Traditional style, 185
Trees in landscaping, 273
Trim, exterior, 180
   interior, 217
   paint for, 211
Types of vacation houses. *See* houses, vacation.

Utilities, 17, *18,* 153, 182, 239-44

Varnish, shingles and shakes, 211
   floor, 217-8
Vinyl floor tile, *203*

Wall, concrete block, 166
   construction of, 165-72
   crib, 167
   load-bearing, 52
   log, 167
   masonry, 166
   stone, 166
   wood-frame, 167
Water, 242-55
   insurance, 4
   shutting off for winter, 292
   table, 17, 248
   testing of, 17, *18,* 242, 249
Water-base paint, exterior, 206-7
   interior, 213-4
Weather considerations, 13, 24
Wells, 244-6
When to build, 59
Wigwam, 184
Wind conditions, 5
Windows, *15,* 175-78
   awning, 177
   bow and bay, 177
   casement, 176
   double-hung wood, 175
   sliding, 176
Winterization, 287-93
Wood, 188
   as a fuel, 237
Wood-frame construction, 167
Wood preservative on shakes and shingles, 211

Zoning, 13, 20